Best of R/

Volume 1

Entitled Parents, Choosing Beggars & Pro Revenge

Edited by Dan Chambers

ISBN (Print): 978-0-620-84512-0
ISBN (E-Book): 978-0-620-84513-7

ABOUT

The internet is a wonderful place, and there are very few corners of it more wonderful than www.Reddit.com

Whether you like games, sowing, sports, fashion, politics, cosplay, trolling or just like to get your news online—Reddit has a community for you. Need help with coding? Can't seem to setup your entertainment system? Got some mystery symptom or need legal advice? There is a place for all of it.

What Reddit also has in abundance, is stories.

Stories from everyday people who encounter humans and situations that will make your head spin. The kind of stories you have nightmares about, that make you grateful that your neighbors are only a "little" weird. Whether to vent their frustration, as a means of catharsis or just to give readers a laugh these beautiful people post hundreds of these strange tales every day.

These humble pages contain just a few gems among an ocean of laughs, cringes and disbelief to be found on Reddit. So if you haven't already, be sure to check out Reddit.

Note:

Stories are published more or less as the original, sans TLDR's, with just a few edits to fix errors, for clarity and to follow a similar style. All titles are published *unchanged* for readers wanting to find them on Reddit.com

ACKNOWLEDGMENTS

Thanks to Meinardt Tydeman from Dalmei for another wonderful cover. To our team of story hunters, fact checkers and proof readers.

To everyone subscribed to r/EntitledParents, r/ChoosingBeggars and r/ProRevenge and especially their moderators for keeping the Subreddits alive and growing. Thank you for your many golds and words of support and encouragement to everyone who has the courage to post.

And of course, our biggest thank you goes out to all the authors of the stories. Without you none of this would be possible, and quite frankly the internet would be just a little bit duller. It was an absolute pleasure working with you all.
A special mention to ImAllergicToFish and Faverules for their altruism and humbleness.

We hope we did your tales justice.

ENTITLED PARENTS

Most people who've had kids for a while will tell you that there is no right way to bring them up. You try your best, try to do better than your parents did. Everyone makes mistakes and there are no perfect parents. No perfect kids either. However, there definitely is a wrong way to bring them up and these stories read like a guide of what not to do.

Rule number four on the r/entitledparents subreddit is DO NOT DEFEND THE ENTITLED PARENTS. Personally, after reading through hundreds of these stories I can't fathom how anyone could conceivably do that. You be the judge.

1

My parents found out that I have money, wants me to give it all to them

So a little backstory.

My parents disowned me for being an atheist (my family is very religious; they will look at you like trash if you say you don't believe in a god). They kicked me out and didn't support me through my last year of college. I haven't spoken to them for almost three years now.

Just a few weeks ago I got word from my cousin that my little sister was hospitalized due to dengue fever so I went to visit her when she was about to be discharged. When I got there it was just my sister in the room. I asked where my parents were and she said that they were trying to raise funds for the hospital bill. Turns out my parents medical insurance didn't cover most of the hospital bill and that left a large out of pocket expense (around twenty six thousand Philippine pesos, and if there are any Filipinos out there you know this a large amount). Fortunately I was able to save up a lot this past year so I went ahead and paid for it.

When my parents came back I told them it's already been paid for and that we're just waiting for the discharge orders. The first questions they ask is why was I there and where did I get the money from. I explained my cousin told me what happened and that I was saving money for my little sister's college.

They didn't even thank me, and the next question they asked is how much money I have saved. I didn't say the amount but they insisted I should give it to them since my sister is living with them. I told them no and that I will give it to my sister personally once she enters college (it's her last year of high school). That wasn't good enough for them. They kept saying "they need the money" but wouldn't specify what it would be for. I didn't budge.

A week passed and they still hadn't stopped bugging me—calling me ungrateful to them as my parents and so on and so forth. They even called my girlfriend and ask her to talk to me about giving them the money.

2

Posted by **SheWhoLovesToDraw**

"Give my Daughter your car! She Deserves it!"

A little background on this story.

First, I have a fairly decent car for it being so old (sixteen year old Dodge Neon SE) and I have zero interest in getting anything different since it's reliable, still gets great gas mileage, is completely paid off and handles great. It's blue with a massive rust spot on the rear passenger side just above the gas tank, but I don't care. (It gives the car character, you know?)

Second, this story takes place in Michigan, where as anyone who lives here or has driven through here knows—the roads here *suck*. Potholes, uneven streets and jagged pavement on every stretch of road you'll ever drive down. Getting a flat tire at least once in your life while living here is both a guarantee and a rite of passage.

The flat tire detail is relevant.

I was driving through town after my shift at work and had to take a really shitty street because that's my route. I do my best to avoid potholes, but I end up striking a few anyway and low and behold my rear driver's side tire takes a hit. I can feel that something's wrong with the tire so I pull off the road into the nearest open drive I could find.

Turns out I picked a used car lot and had plenty of room to inspect the damage. When I step out of the car to look at the tire another car pulls into the lot behind me and proceeds to park on the other side. I noticed that the tire was low, but not flat because fortunately the pothole only loosened the seal on the stem valve and I could fix it with the can of 'fix-a-flat' that I keep in my trunk.

While I'm fussing with my tire the dealership owner comes out to greet me, most likely assuming I'm there to either trade in my car or shop around. When he sees my tire is low he insists I slowly pull my car further away from the side of the road and up toward the front of the dealership building out of safety concerns. I agree and move my car where instructed.

Turns out I was being watched by a dreaded Entitled Parent and her demonic spawn.

Not long after I get my car moved, the dealership owner is lending me a hand and helping with my tire—making sure the valve was secured and the pressure was stable. I thanked him for his help and proceeded to sit back down in my car. As I put the key in the ignition I hear something bang against my window and look up to see a woman, the stereotypical 'Karen', trying to get my attention.

I roll my window down to see what she wants. "Yeah? What's up?"

"Are you through yet?

"Am I . . . what?" I ask in confusion.

"*Through,*" the Entitled Parent repeats. "Are your through, because my daughter's been waiting long enough!"

I look past her and see her sixteen year old daughter dressed in a dark mini-skirt, white tank top (that showed everything) and four inch heels. (This is February BTW) She was also wearing so much cheap make-up you'd think she was auditioning for a role as "The Joker".

"Waiting for what?" I ask.

"Don't act cute! She needs her turn, you've taken up enough of our time."

"What're you talking about?"

"Are you stupid?" she asks. "Your test drive is over, now it's Entitled Brat's turn!"

The Entitled Brat is standing behind her mother, arms crossed over her chest and giving me a smug *Wow, are all you 'commoners' so stupid?* type of grin on her arrogant face.

"Oh," I figure it out quickly and try to diffuse the situation, "I wasn't on a test drive, I own—"

"—I said get out!" the Entitled Parent screams.

"This is *my* car."

"No it's not!" she insists. "I just saw you pull back into the lot. We were behind you the whole time so don't try to lie to me!"

"I wasn't—"

"You didn't even go inside the building to sign the papers, so I *know* you're lying to me! You didn't buy this car, you're just being a stubborn little bitch."

"No, this is my car. I have the regis—"

"—What the fuck is wrong with you? Get out *now!*"

"This is my car!"

"No it's not! My daughter wants it and I'm going to buy it for her *right* now." She tried to pull open my door, but thankfully I locked it when I got inside. "Give me the key!"

Before I had the chance to say anything else she reached through my window and made a grab for the key in the ignition (the key that was on a keyring with my apartment key and four other keychains, so clearly not the dealership's key). When she tried to pull it out I grabbed her arm and pushed her back. "Get away!"

"You little bitch!" she screamed. "You just assaulted me!"

I quickly roll up my window, ready to drive off when I see the dealership owner returning.

"Ma'am, what's going on?" he asks.

"This little whore just assaulted me!" the Entitled Parent yells. "Call the police. She attacked me because I told her to let my daughter have a test drive and now she's trying to steal the car!"

The man looks at me, then at my worn out, dirty car with the faded bumper sticker on the trunk and gives the woman the classic *are you serious right now?* stare. "Ma'am, this car isn't for sale. This is *her* car."

"No it's not!" she insists stubbornly. "Until she signs the paper it's *not* hers and my daughter wants to drive it! She just got her license and I promised her I'd get her a blue car. This is the only blue car in the lot!"

It was not. There was another blue car parked behind her, and yes, her sixteen year old daughter who just got her license was going to test drive a car in heels. Double WTF?

"Ma'am, this car isn't mine to sell. It *already* belongs to her."

She wouldn't be dissuaded. "No it doesn't! I *saw* her drive the car onto the lot and I *saw* you telling her to pull up to the building! Stop trying to lie to me!"

"She had a low tire," the dealer says, "she pulled off—"

"Why won't you let my daughter have her turn? She deserves her turn! Is it because my daughter isn't all slutted up like this whore?"

Remember what the daughter was wearing? I'm in blue jeans, tennis shoes, a baggy shirt with Kirby (from Nintendo) on it and a green jacket over top. The only skin visible is on my hands, neck and face.

The dealer tries again. "Ma'am, stop. I'm going to have to ask you to leave."

"No! My daughter *needs* this car! I promised her and all you're doing is wasting my time!"

"I'm asking you nicely to leave before I call the cops."

"You do that and I'm telling the cops that this bitch assaulted me, pushed my daughter and that you're selling stolen cars! Now, give my daughter this car right now or else!"

She actually said "or else", like a damn cartoon villain.

The dealer doesn't budge. "Ma'am. Leave."

"This is ridiculous!" She pulled her phone from her purse and proceeded to call the cops herself. "You're going to regret being so disrespectful to me! All you had to do was sell me this car, but *no,* you decided this whore was better than my daughter! My daughter deserves this car!"

I know I'm not in the wrong, but I'm still nervous. I look at the dealer through the windshield and he gives me a look that says *everything will be fine, watch this.*

About five minutes later a patrol car pulls up and the officer approaches the dealer.

Before he even has the chance to ask any questions the Entitled Parent starts shrieking at him at full volume. "I want that bitch arrested! She assaulted me and my daughter and she's trying to steal my daughter's car!"

The cop is unfazed and just looks at me, then over to the owner without blinking. "Hey Steve, is this true?"

"Not a word of it," Steve replied. "And if you want you can check the lot's security cameras Tom".

They knew each other by name.

The Entitled Parent is fuming while the Entitled Brat is just rolling her eyes like we were boring her or some shit. "Why don't you believe me? You're not seriously going to take her word over mine. Just *look* at her!"

"Ma'am, I need to get both sides of the story," the cop warned. "Now, you said she tried to steal—"

"Yes. That's *my* daughter's car!"

"Alright, fine. That's easy enough to prove." The cop walked over to the passenger's side of the door, on the opposite side from where the Entitled Parent was still seething, and motioned for me to open the door. I did and he of course asked for my identification, registration and proof of insurance. It didn't take the cop long to notice my name on the license and the name on the registration (which was also dated from almost two years ago) are a match. He just nods, hands me back my stuff and closes the door. "Ma'am, that's her car."

"Not possible! She just got here, she couldn't have signed the papers! Why are you all against my daughter? She *needs* a car!"

The cop is unfazed. "Ma'am, you do realize it's a crime to try filing a false police report? This car isn't stolen and I seriously doubt she assaulted you. I'm going to look at the cameras, and if I find that you're lying to me—"

Before he could finish the sentence the Entitled Parent promptly grabbed Entitled Brat's arm and began pulling her along. "Fuck this place! All these cars are pieces of shit anyway! My daughter deserves *better* than anything that slut would ever drive!"

The cop sticks around until the Entitled Parent leaves, apologizes to me for the disturbance and wishes me a good day. Before leaving he said bye to the dealer, again calling him by his first name and was on his way.

"Don't worry about her," the dealer said. "I don't think she'll be back. And if she does show up again my brother Tom will be back too."

After slipping me a business card, joking that if I ever needed another car in the near future, he assured me that no crazy people were hiding in the trunk.

I thanked the man for coming to my rescue, drove off and I've been trying to figure out why my old car was so important to the Entitled Parent ever since.

Seriously, it's not that great a car; old, losing it's pep and needing some TLC. But I still love my 'blue-bastard!'

3

EP wants me to shovel her driveway for free, and put my dog down. I get hilarious revenge!

I live in a middle-middle upper class neighborhood, everyone is very friendly and it's right next to a school. My neighborhood is in the east side of Pennsylvania, and if anyone lives near there you will know about the snow. We got about 6 inches of snow, so of course school was cancelled. I also have a service dog.

I woke up about seven in the morning and decided to go outside and play with my dog. We were having fun running around when I noticed my neighbor trying to get in his car. Now I don't know what happened, and it's not my business, but my neighbor is wheelchair bound. He drives his car with those special handles you attach to the pedals.

Anyway, I noticed him trying and failing to get through the 6 inches of snow on his driveway, so I decided to help him out. I went to my shed, grabbed a shovel and some rock salt. I walked over and offered to shovel his driveway so he could go wherever he needs to be. My neighbor accepted and thanked me for being so helpful, then he went back inside. Over the course of the next hour or so I shoveled his driveway and salted it. My dog sat at the edge the whole time, ready for action like the good girl she is. After I was done I informed my neighbor, who thanked me again, and I started walking away.

The Entitled Mom was walking down the street and noticed me while I was finishing up. She decided to strike. "Hey, so I noticed you shoveled Bob's driveway and I was wondering if you could shovel mine?"

"Sure," I replied. "I'll do it for ten dollars."

"But you shoveled his driveway for free!"

"If you haven't noticed, he can't move his legs or shovel the driveway himself."

"Well I have children and I need to drive to the store to feed them!"

"What's stopping you from shoveling?" I asked. "You seem perfectly fine to me."

"Can't you just help out a mother?"

"Give me ten dollars and I will."

She lost it. "You fucking millennials have no respect for anyone. I am a hard working mother and you have no right to refuse what I tell you to do."

This bitch has the *audacity* to try to grab my arm and pull me.

I yanked my arm away. "What the fuck is wrong with you! Get away from me!"

My dog is very protective of me. At this point she stands between us and growls at the lady.

"Your dog is crazy!" the Entitled mom shrieks. "She's going to attack me! You need to put down that monster!" *(Editor's note: the "monster" is an adorable fluffy white poodle)*

My dog is a monster huh? Okay then.

I yelled, "Sic 'em girl" and the dog lets out a single bark, not even that scary.

The Entitled Mother runs for her fucking life.

I took off dogs vest so she's not on duty and threw a stick near the Entitled Parent. The mother doesn't see it.

"Get it girl."

Dog takes off towards the stick, Entitled Parent turns around and a look of sheer terror fills her face as she sees my dog barreling towards her.

I'm laughing my ass off.

I went home after that and gave her extra treato's and pats for doing a big protec.

Hope everyone near me has a wonderful snow day!

4

Pink is for girls

Today the barber shop where I work wasn't very busy. We had only given cuts to four people and the other barber went home after nobody came for an hour, which was irresponsible but I can't blame him.

Then the fifth customer walks in, a woman with her son. The son looked about fifteen and the mother looked around forty. They sit down and I give the boy a haircut. At the end of the cut the boy asks for a little bit of pink dye in the front of his hair (the mom wasn't watching, she was on her phone) so I did what he asked.

When I was finished I told the woman the total and she looks at her son. "What the hell is that? Why there is pink in my son's hair?"

"Mo—" the boy began but was cut off by his mother ignoring him and turning to me.

"What the fuck is your problem? You aren't getting paid for ruining my son's hair."

"I'm sorry ma'am but—"

"—Mom I asked for it," the boy says.

The Entitled Mom looks at the boy with evil eyes and I knew something was going to happen. I have to say I really appreciate that boy sticking up for me because I expected he'd say nothing and normally I don't know what to say in these situations so brownie points to him.

"Why?" she screeched. "Pink is for girls, not boys!"

She's shouting now, basically what I expected. I mean what else could she do? Sue him for having pink in his hair?

The boy has had enough. "You know what? I'm sick of your shit mom. You literally don't respect anything I do! If I hang out with the disabled at school you will force me to hang around with the people who pick on them and when my girlfriend bought me a shirt with a pink heart on it you throw it in the garbage. You are so fucking lazy. You make me and dad do everything around the house. Fuck you mom!"

The boy then stormed out of the shop and the mother left to chase him without paying.

I was shocked and confused but the boy returned a few minutes later and tossed twenty dollars in to the shop. He didn't even step inside, just opened the door and threw it in. I think his crazy mom was chasing him. I was still in shock and felt bad for the kid.

I never saw them again and I don't work at the barbershop anymore.

5

"THIS IS AMERICA! SPEAK ENGLISH OR GET OUT!" EP falsely accuses me and yells for not speaking English with my friend in a cafe

I live in a predominately white, suburban neighborhood in America. This neighborhood is so disproportionately white that I would say ninety percent of the people I know are white, and I will seldom see more than ten non-white people in a day. Ninety nine point nine percent of the people in this neighborhood are very nice and caring!

It's just the zero point zero one percent that this story is about.

I am a Korean-American teen living in America who emigrated from Korea when I was around six. I.E. speak English fluently, albeit with a moderate Korean accent, which I have had pointed out to me over the years, often in a derogatory way. It doesn't help that I'm in a neighborhood where people aren't used to it, and I've been teased before. Doesn't really bother me, as I can't really refute. I have two names, my American and my Korean. This is important later on.

Now to bring in my friend, Jia. I've known her for a while, and she recently moved to America from Korea. Key word: recently. She knows practically *no* English aside from what schools taught her back in Korea. Her vocabulary consisted of simple words like "sorry, hello, how are you, please," etc. She's not very confident about speaking English to other people, and naturally doesn't say much for fear of not knowing what to say.

Because I wanted to hang out with her and talk I invited Jia to go to a Café which had another Korean person working there. I was good friends with this person and I wanted Jia to meet more Korean people so she could talk to more people than just me.

[Author's Note: Dialogue here will be roughly translated for convenience, so it might sound a bit awkward. When the conversation is Korean, it will be in italics]

Me and my friend were just talking about regular stuff, mostly "how have you been?" and "long time no see!" talk, as it's the first time I've seen her in a while between the move and all the unpacking.

"I don't think I could ever get used to America . . ." Jia said. *"Everything's so*

inconvenient here. Getting used to it would be like plucking a star out of the sky (a Korean saying for impossible). Besides, why is the internet so slow here? I could take a shower in the time it takes for me to search something."

At this point the Entitled Kid comes walking along and notices us talking. He stares at us while walking with two coffees in his hands before coming to a stop at our table.

"You should speak English," he says suddenly.

Taken aback, I say, "I'm sorry, what?"

"You should speak English," he repeats. "This is America, not China."

"Why do we have to speak English here?" I asked. "We aren't even speaking to you."

Jia, not understanding the situation asks me in Korean what we did wrong.

"Nothing," I reply. *"It's just this kid wants us to speak English."*

"Are you making fun of me?" the kid demands.

Jia looks up. "Sorry . . . I don't speak English very good."

I laughed playfully. *"Hey, you've gotten good at English."*

Too late I realized my mistake.

Convinced that we were making fun of him the kid stomps away, visibly angry.

"Why'd you apologize?" I asked Jia. *"Don't apologize to people like him! We were doing nothing wrong, don't worry."*

"Is this common in America?"

I started to reassure her that this was the first time this happened to me and it is not at all common when the Entitled Parent showed up, kid at her side. "I hear you've been making fun of my kid?"

I turned to her. "No, we weren't. We were just speaking to each other."

"I'm not someone you want to lie to," she threatened, "You were making fun of my kid in Chinese, weren't you!?

"I told you, we weren't," I replied firmly.

"Stop with this bullshit! I know both of you can speak English and deliberately chose to speak Chinese in front of my kid. What were you saying?"

"Ma'am, my friend doesn't speak English. She moved from Korea a month ago and barely knows it. That's why we were talking in Korean."

Entitled Kid then points to Jia. "No, you're wrong! I heard her say sorry to me! In English! I know she can speak English!"

15

At this point Jia had enough and I could tell she was on the verge of tears. Imagine someone accusing you and yelling at you in a language that you can't even understand and not being able to defend yourself.

The sight of this made me especially angry and I panicked, lashing out. "I know how to say '*hola*'. Does that mean I know all of fucking Spanish? Please leave us alone."

We were now causing a commotion overhead by other people at the Cafe.

The mother balked. "You don't speak to me like that with that language. Apologize to me right now!"

"What do we have to apologize for" I asked angrily. "We did nothing wrong! Why do I have to speak English just because you're here?"

"You will *not* disrespect me or my kid in this way! This is America, you should be speaking English. *English!* Do you know how rude it is to everyone around you? If you want to speak Chinese, go back to China!"

Jia started to cry a bit.

One of the staff, the Korean one I talked about earlier, finally overheard and came over.

"Ma'am, is there a problem here?" the Café worker asked.

She nodded. "Yes, these two kids are making fun of my child in Chinese."

"Do you speak Chinese?"

"No," she replied, "but they should be speaking English! They were laughing at my kid! They both speak English! They should get kicked out of the Cafe for this!

"Hey, were you making fun of this kid?" the Café worker asked us gently in a gentle tone.

"No," Jia said quickly, relieved she could finally say something. *"We really weren't. He approached us first."*

"Are you siding with her in this?" the mother asked in astonishment.

"Ma'am," the Café worker began calmly, "you know people have the right to speak whatever language they want here . . . right?"

"They have the right to make fun of my kid in whatever language they want? Even when she knows English? If they want to say something, say it to my face."

The Café worker looked at Jia. *"Do you speak English? You're much more comfortable in Korean, right? What happened? Don't worry about language, I'm Korean too. Just tell me what happened."*

Jia proceeded to explain everything that happened and when she was done the Café worker turned back to the mother. "Ma'am, Jia here is saying that your kid was the one who bothered them first—"

"That's a complete lie!"

The Café worker shook her head. "Instead of yelling at kids, *kids*, over this why don't we find some tangible evidence instead of some claims? I can check the cameras for you. Y'know, just as a double-check?"

The Entitled Parent was adamant, but the kid visibly reacted to this.

"How dare you accuse my kid of instigating this situation! Let me see the evidence right now!" she demanded.

The Entitled Kid leaned over and whispered something to the parent.

"Miss, if you keep this up we might have to call the police for harassment and disturbance of public peace," the Café worker said.

It was then that Entitled Parent suddenly changed her mind.

"Look lady," the parent muttered. "I don't have time for this. I have a meeting to get to. This was a huge waste of time. Goodbye."

It was obvious she was just trying to diffuse the situation, but that didn't stop her from glaring at me before she left.

We didn't try and pursue her, as we didn't want to poke the fire and ruin our day more than it had already been ruined.

On the bright side, I never saw her again.

6

My friends tits are offensive to EM

Me and my best friends where at the beach, just chilling. One thing I need to point out is my best friend is on the big breasted side of the spectrum. So, like any big breasted woman, bikinis are a nightmare to her. She is always getting stared at, and that makes her really uncomfortable.

We were in a more secluded part of the beach, having just swam and we decided to sit a bit. When we come back to our chairs a family has settled down near us. The mom was in her late thirties, the dad was in his early fifties and they had a child with them, a nine-ish year old boy.

We didn't pay any mind to them, just sat in our chairs and talked for a bit but I did notice the dad looking at my friend. I ignored it. I decide to get something to drink (there was a bar nearby), I asked my friend if she wanted something and she replied a lemonade. I headed to the bar and while I waited in line the Entitled Mother comes to talk to me.

"Hi," she said. "I saw that you and your friend are nearby me and my family."

I just nodded.

"I think your friend is really beautiful, but she is showing too much cleavage."

I looked at her, trying to think how to respond to this. "Well, she can't be faulted for being born with big breasts can she?"

She looked at me like she was expecting me to agree with her. ""Well she could not use a bikini that small," she replied in a somewhat annoyed voice.

"She can do whatever she wants lady."

She became red at that. I don't think that this woman has ever heard someone disagree with her before. "She is looking like a slut! My child will be traumatized!"

I looked back to where my friend is sitting. I have a clear view of her and the mother's family. Her child is making sand castles, a cute view I might add, and her husband is starring hard at my friend who was applying sunscreen at the time. So, the problem was not her child—it was her husband.

"Well I can't do much lady, now please leave me alone."

Finally it was my turn in line, so I pick my drinks and ignore the Entitled mother who wasn't happy about it.

"Don't you dare ignore me young man. I'm not finished!"

I just look at her and took a sip of my drink before saying, "Lady, your kid isn't even looking at my friend. Your husband on other hand . . ."

I pointed at her husband who was staring at my friend with hungry eyes.

She looked shocked, and just starting walking to her husband. I go back to my friend, gave her drink and sat beside her—watching the wife furiously whispering to her husband. Not long after, my friend and I decided to leave.

I didn't tell my friend about the crazy lady—she has enough confidence issues. At least I didn't see this family ever again.

(Editor's note: When we contacted ImAllergicToFish he insisted we waive his portion of the sales because "he didn't deserve it for the story", allowing us to divide it between the other authors. You will have to look far and wide to meet a friendlier and humble man. Sir, you are most worthy.)

7

Posted by **Logan Farmer (Nagol93)**

Can you use your vacation days to watch our dog while we take a real vacation?

This happened about three or four years after I moved out of my parent's house and have been living independently. One day I get this string of texts from my mom.

"Hay, how have you been doing? What you up to two weeks from now?" she asked.

"I've been doing alright, I've started lifting weights and exercising more. I don't think I'm doing anything too exciting next week. Why you ask?" I texted back.

"Perfect! Me and the boyfriend are going on a trip and need you to house sit and watch the dogs for us."

"Sorry but I can't just leave for a week,"

"Please, the dogs miss you and I'd really hate to put them in the kennel."

"Sorry but I have a job, I can't just go missing for a week."

"Why can't you drive to work from my house?"

"Because it's a two and a half hour commute each way."

"You have vacation days, right? Just use them."

"No."

"Please. I'd feel really bad about putting Fluffy in the kennel. You

know how much she hates it."

"You obviously don't feel that bad about doing it."

Then I hear nothing from her until the day before they have their trip.

"Hay, we're leaving for our trip today and I was wondering when you were going to be here? I want to show you some things before we leave."

"What part of our last conversation gave you any idea that I agreed to this?"

"That's very rude of you and no way to speak to your mother. Now can we expect you here by 5?"

And at that point I just put my phone on silent and stopped talking to her.

My landlord doesn't allow pets, so I couldn't keep them for a week anyway. Also the dogs went to the kennel and came out just fine. However this all happened a while ago and both dogs have passed since then. One to stomach cancer, the other to old age :(

I'll miss you two.

8

Posted by **Iko On**

The PC Trilogy

I worked in a retail computer store where I am a part time technician but also deal with customers with regards to sales, etc.

A while back we had this Entitled Mother and kid come in to buy a new computer for the kid. We discuss some options in their price range and end up selling EK a mid-range gaming computer. This happened on a weekend as it was the only time I ever worked, as I was part-time.

Fast forward to the next week. I come in to work and see the Entitled Kid's rig on the table by the other tech work. My colleague calls me over, as I was the only 'avid' gamer in the shop, and tells me that this is my baby seeing as I sold EK the rig and I would know how to fix some game related issues (little did I know at the time that he was avoiding the screaming banshee and rather passed the work on to me).

I didn't mind working on it at all because I could have some fun while working as I had to test why the game wasn't working the on kid's computer. The game in question was *Tom Clancy's Ghost Recon Online*. This happened during the early release of the game and being a free to play game there were bound to be bugs. The first few times the game crashed on startup, sometimes mid-match and other times just refused to even start.

About an hour into testing the computer the Entitled Mother storms in. I don't exactly remember the dialogue as this was a few years ago. She basically shouted at me about the "useless" computer I sold her.

At this point I am trying to explain to her I did not know why the game isn't working, as I still haven't gotten a clue myself yet—many other people are having the same problems. She wasn't having any of it.

She told me to refund her for the computer as we sold her useless trash and the kid "can't use it anymore".

She was red in the face when I told her, "First off, our store has a 'no refund' policy which you can clearly see on the wall behind me. Secondly there is nothing wrong with the computer we sold you but rather the game itself is broken."

It was after I made it clear that the game wasn't working that she then requested a refund . . . for a free to play game?

It turns out the kid spun some story about how he bought the game. At first I thought he bought in game currency, but only later realized he actually bought hacks.

She was livid that we never made it clear that there is a "no refund" policy and stormed out. Eventually, after a whole day of working on it, I got this game to work (not for long because 2-3 weeks later a new update got released and the game broke again).

Lo and behold Entitled Mother returned, screaming at me again about the broken game which turned out to be the kid actually being banned for hacking.

I had been working on this computer for a full day and she was furious when I told her that the hours of labor I worked would only cost her seventeen dollars (which was very cheap considering). She basically stated that the computer was garbage and that it should have worked on day one. She eventually paid and left the store never to return again.

Or so I hoped.

Three weeks after the initial fix it was the start of the new month and everyone had their salaries paid in. This means our shop was very busy—we barely had enough reps to deal with customers I was busy talking to a customer at the tech desk with a laptop that had a lot of issues from emails not working to USB ports malfunctioning. Even blue screens of death.

In walks Entitled Mother, no kid and no PC. I thought she may have just been shopping around for new games or a keyboard or something for the kid. She walks up to the tech desk and I quickly greet her with a "Hi Entitled Mother, I'll be with you in a minute."

She stood there, arms crossed tapping her foot as if I was inconveniencing her by talking to a customer. About five minutes after I booked in the laptop and printed the necessary work orders the Entitled Mother favored me with this funny look and then proceeded to say, "Um, I've been waiting for forever. Are you going to come pick up this computer from my car or not?"

I just looked at her with a confused expression. She then told me she phoned the shop, that my work colleague answered and she said that she was on her way to drop of the kid's computer, again. Apparently she'd been parked outside our shop waiting in the disabled parking outside our front door for fifteen minutes. Customers did this often. We we're so busy that my colleague afterwards had to apologize because we didn't have the time to look outside for a car to pick up a computer or inform me she was on her way.

I went outside to fetch the machine. The Entitled mother was annoyed again, asking why the game doesn't work. After a few minutes of her trying to explain what her son told her I said I can figure it out and have a look at it. This time she knew to ask what the labor cost would be due to the previous event. Knowing how stingy she is I told her no more than twenty dollars. She seemed fine with this if it was the games fault again this time. After printing out papers she left.

This is where the "fun" begins.

We couldn't access the account for some reason. I just remember having difficulty opening Steam. At this point I just thought he forgot his details and we did the whole 'steam password reset' thing. After an hour of no results I write an email to Steam support asking for help with the account. The next day steam wrote back with something along the lines of: "This Steam account has violated the terms of service and is therefore banned", a lengthy email detailing why the account got banned and that it could not be retrieved. I was shocked.

The kid tried to add cracked games to the Steam library. There were no actual bought games in his library and I saw the icons on the desktop for a few games that cost well over twenty dollars. He'd bought aim hacking software for Ghost Recon online. Knowing now why the game "Wasn't working" I called the mother to ask her and the kid to come to the shop so I can explain why the game isn't working. This didn't seem like something I could say over the phone.

I don't know exactly why his steam account itself was banned. Usually a VAC ban only affects the game you cheated in, but I think he may have even tried to crack Steam to get games for free. I don't have a lot of experience with Steam bans so forgive me for being a bit hazy on the details, and this was around five years ago after all.

A while later they both entered the store on a Sunday, thankfully a lot quieter than the last visit. I had printed out the response I got from Steam and I told her that the kid had been using illegal software that he bought with her credit card without permission and that Steam had banned his account. I handed her the printed out mail so she could confirm that I wasn't lying or making any excuses. The look on the Entitled Kid's face was priceless. At this point he knew he royally fucked up and his face went white.

She turned over to him to ask what this was all about and he just nodded and said "sorry". She was once again livid, asking how he could just use her card without her permission. How he could buy illegal software. How he could lie to her face about all of it. The kid was now bawling his eyes out.

This is where I started getting some respect for Entitled Mother—she didn't even complain about the labor price. She asked us to keep the PC in the shop for the whole week so EK could learn a lesson and clear it of all the illegal software. She was even fine with paying for the extra labor hours (at the end we did a full new windows install as the cracks and hacks had tons of viruses included so we spent a lot more time working on the computer).

Unfortunately, the respect didn't last for long.

Sometime later the Entitled Mother came in with her work computer, the kid's gaming rig and 2 tablets. We had to do some routine virus removal for the two computers and one of the tablets didn't want to work properly.

Our company policy dictates a minimum of seventeen dollar's labor per device, per hour. That means we could have charge her around seventy dollars for the labor we did. The two tablets were easily sorted out after we did factory restoring and reinstalling of most of their usual apps. The kid's gaming rig, again, had a few viruses on it because of his torrenting of movies, music, games, etc. (the usual shit that comes with trying to download torrents). Her work computer was fucked. We had to do a full on wipe the machine, do virus scans on our expendable tech PC of all the backed up data, clear everything and restore her data virus free. This took us about two whole days working on her machine alone.

That Monday I had to go back to university but was filled in by my coworker. My boss, knowing how unreasonable this Entitled Mother was, told us it's fine to charge her a measly thirty five dollars for all the work which for our shop was still a lot for tech work. When she came in on Monday to fetch everything she went red with rage after my coworker notified her what the labor would be.

Now thirty five dollars for all the work we did on her devices is nothing.

Any other shop would have charged well over a hundred for all the time and energy spent. She kept shouting, in front of customers, about how unacceptable our rates were and that she refuses to pay a whole thirty five dollars for the work as we "work on multiple client's machines at the same time".

We have a switch (I can't remember the name of it) that you can plug four computers into and flip the screen between the four PC's so you can easily multi-task and work on more than one computer on the same screen (most tech shops have this). Usually when one machine is busy doing something like a backup or virus scan we switch to other computers to keep working. She threw a fit that we didn't prioritize her computer (which we actually did, it took preference over any other computers we had plugged in) and also stated that kid's machine was a quick fix plus the tablets we just 'reset'. Any shop would do that for free.

Now my boss, reasonable as he is and wanting to get this screaming hag as he called her out of the shop, begrudgingly lowered the price to seventeen dollars, let her pay and told her that if she is unhappy with our low priced services she can go somewhere else. My boss doesn't take shit from anyone, not even a customer. We usually did anything we could to keep a customer coming back, but he wasn't having her chasing away potential customers with her banshee screaming.

I don't remember seeing her again after this so I'm glad. I think she was too embarrassed when she realized how cheap our prices really were and didn't want to admit defeat.

(Editor's note: this story was originally three different posts, "EM blames us for a free to play game not working", "EK gets steam ban, EM blames computer we sold them." and "EM refuses to pay for low labor (Part 3)", heavily edited in to one flowing piece.)

9

EM almost kills her child because she wanted him to ride a ride he wasn't allowed to, tries to press assault charges against me

When I was sixteen I worked at the amusement park in my city. It wasn't a big one, but it wasn't small either. Most of our rides were aimed towards elementary school children, though we had a few for the older kids as well. I was a rides operator, and that day I was assigned to a ride designed for older kids. We had to measure the kids and they couldn't go on if they were under the height requirements no matter what. Even if they had a parent with them because it was a ride that only had a bar that went across your stomach. Someone too small could easily fall off.

Entitled Mother and her Entitled Brat are in line, and I can already tell the kid is going to be too short to ride without having to measure him. He's pretty far back, one or two runs before he makes it on, so after I'm done loading I tell the mother that her kid is too short for the ride and that they should go try the smaller version of it on the other side of the park.

She looks at me with the dirtiest stare ever and just says we're going to wait here."

I have to run my ride because I need to meet certain times so I don't argue. Time goes by and she's finally at the start of the line. I measure her kid, and of course he's like six inches shorter than the height requirement.

"I'm sorry ma'am," I say, "but your child is too short to ride this ride. I would recommend going over to the smaller version near the entrance of the park."

"No, it's fine. I'm with him and I'll hold him."

She then tries to shove me out of the way, but I'm standing my ground. "I'm really sorry ma'am, but we don't allow people under the height limit on ride this ride. The safeties we have on it just won't hold someone too small, and your kid could fall off."

She asks to speak to my manager.

I get asked that quite a lot by entitled parents, so I give them a call and tell her to wait on the side while I load my ride. She gets very offended, saying that she shouldn't have to wait longer for her kid to ride because I couldn't do my job. At this point I just kind of ignore her and move on.

The ride runs, my team lead gets there and talks with her. He tells her that he's really sorry but that I'm right and her child can't ride. The brat starts throwing a tantrum, and I mean he's rolling on the concrete like a piece of bacon in a frying pan. I'm trying my hardest not to laugh.

My manager apologizes, offers her a "skip the line" ticket for the ride he's allowed to go on at the entrance and leaves. The mother is trying to calm the brat down by talking quietly to him. He gets up suddenly, all smiling and happy and stands next to the gates, watching me. I'm not thinking too much of it and start loading my ride again, which was significantly less busy and I have a couple of empty seats on it.

As I'm doing my security checks and getting ready to run it the mother taps me on the shoulder and thanks me for my help, which I found extremely odd. I turn around to tell her that it's really no problem and she starts apologizing and telling me that she shouldn't have acted the way she did and blah, blah, blah. I'm completely stunned and not really sure how to react so I tell her it's no problem and to enjoy the rest of her day.

I look back at my ride and realize that the brat isn't standing next to the fence anymore.

I'm starting to get weird vibes. I look around for him and he's not anywhere to be seen. I look to the mother again who has her phone out with her camera pointing at the ride, and that's when I knew.

I take my keys out the ride and start walking towards it. It's kind of a "swing" type thing so I couldn't see the back from where I was standing, but I knew damn well the brat had snuck on. The mother starts panicking, asking me what I'm doing and why I'm not running the ride. I completely ignore her and walk to the back of the ride. Lo and behold, the brat is sitting there and almost shits himself when he sees me walking towards him.

He didn't have the bar properly locked at all, and would've flown right out as soon as I started the ride. Now I am mad, and I mean mad. I could've gone to jail for manslaughter. I just look at him, and very sternly tell him to get off my ride. He tells me he can't and he needs help, which is fair. I mean I don't even know how he managed to get on in the first place, but I grab him and put him down.

Crying, he starts sprinting towards his mom. As he's running he trips and falls down on his face. When he gets up his nose is all bloody and his knees are skinned, which is when I knew I was completely and utterly fucked.

The Entitled Mother starts screaming like a banshee at the sight. As I'm running towards the kid to make sure he's not dead and to help him up she runs towards me, slaps me hard across the face and yells for security. I'm absolutely and completely stunned at this point. Some security guards must've heard her screaming at the top of her lungs because they come running.

"What's going on here?" one of the guards asks.

"This girl assaulted my son! She threw him off the ride unto the pavement!"

"Excuse me?" I sputter. Did she really want them to believe I just vaulted her child ten feet away from where he was sitting?

"It's true!" the mother insists. "She punched me too."

"Do you want us to call the police?" the guard asks her.

"Yes! You need to arrest her! She's mentally unstable."

I'm just dumbfounded at this point. My manager gets to the ride and asks what the hell is going on and I tell him everything that happened in between sobs. But there's one thing the mother forgot to take into account—the fifteen people on the ride who saw everything.

They tell the police, the security guards, my manager and everyone else what happened. Quickly realizing her error, the mother just started running with her kid in tow as soon as she saw people asking questions.

They caught her pretty quickly and I pressed assault charges against her. Needless to say, I handed in my resignation that same day.

10

Posted by **flyting1881**

EM wants me to lie about witnessing sexual harassment to protect her son

I teach eighth grade, and a few months ago I had a female student come up to me in private and tell me that a male student in her class was sexually harassing her.

She shows me text messages that he has sent her, detailing highly graphic sexual things he wants to do to her. She also tells me some of the things he's said to her when they are in the halls. The young woman has asked him to stop repeatedly but he is still doing it, and she wants me to help keep him away from her in my class.

Before I file a report to have guidance and admin investigate the issue I spend a class period keeping a close eye on the two of them to see if I can confirm or deny anything she's saying. Once I'm looking for it I observe the male student doing things like licking his lips at her from the other side of the room, hovering around her and finding reasons to walk past her desk. I personally overhear him make a sexual comment about her to another student.

Based on what I've seen I go ahead with referring the boy to admin for sexual harassment and make contact with parents of both students to inform them that the issue will be investigated by the school and possible disciplinary action will be taken. I don't make direct contact with the boy's mother but I leave her a voicemail and ask that she call me back. The next day I'm in my planning period and I get a call from the office saying there's a parent there for a meeting.

Our policy is that parent meetings must be scheduled in advance and logged with the office. I don't have any meetings scheduled today, but I have time so I decide to go and see what's up.

It turns out to be the male student's mother in the office. She very nicely asks if we can talk face to face about what's going on, and for some dumb reason I agree even though usually we like to have another teacher or staff member present for meetings. So we go in a conference room and I go over the allegations (avoiding names). I tell her that a female student has accused her son of sexual harassment and I saw enough evidence in class to refer it to the office for investigation.

"Now what exactly did you hear?" she asks. "Because I know my son. He would never harass a girl. He might say something stupid that got taken the wrong way, but that's just not who he is. So what exactly did you hear him say? I want to know what this girl is saying about him."

"I saw him licking his lips at her and overheard him say to another boy that he wanted to 'ride that ass all night'."

"What do you mean licking his lips? He gets chapped lips. He might not be doing it to harass some girl. She can't just say things about him and try to ruin his life - I know my son and he is not that kind of person, no matter what some girl says."

"Well, admin and guidance are going to investigate and based on what they find they'll be in touch with you," I reply.

"Wait, what did you tell them? You can't just go and say my son is harassing girls' based on what one person says," she says sternly. "He's already been suspended twice, and now you're going to get him expelled just because some girl wants to get him in trouble for no reason?"

Now I'm thinking ugh, why did I do this. The mom is getting worked up, I have no one else there and my next class starts soon. I repeat that I just reported the things the girl said and the things I saw, and that it'll be investigated. I reiterate that I'm not the one making any final decision and if she has an issue she needs to talk to the principal.

"Well the principle hates my son so she's not going to listen," she whines. "You need to go and tell them that this is all nonsense. You saw him licking his lips because they were chapped. I'm not going to have all this 'harassment' bullshit."

"Again, if you have an issue I'm not the one to talk to. I just reported what I saw. They'll look into it."

"But you didn't see anything and you need to tell them that. I'm telling you - I know my son, and you've got this all wrong. If he gets expelled because you don't know what you saw it's going to be your fault."

I eventually talk her down enough to get her to leave, then report to admin that the parent is hostile about the accusations and go about my day. They end up investigating and find hard evidence that he was actually sexually harassing three different girls.

Boy got expelled.

11

Posted by **ProfessionalDish**

EM thinks we're a daycare. Welp, her child is now gone.

I used to work in a small chain of bookstores. We'd sell books, pens, paper and so on. It was a quirky little store, straight out of a romantic love novella (or a Stephen King book, if you prefer). This happened a few years ago and I'm reconstructing it from my memory. While trying to be as accurate as possible I can't guarantee it.

Early in the morning an Entitled Mother walks into the store with a little girl. She looks around, then asks me if I could watch her child.

"Oh no, I'm terrible with children, sorry," I reply.

The mother tells me that it's not for that long and I shouldn't make such a fuss about it. I still politely refuse. It's not my job to watch children, and I'm afraid I'll do something wrong.

What happens? She leaves the store, and who do I find hidden in the corner? The little girl who seems to be rather shy and almost fearful.

This happened back in a time before everyone had smartphones. The kid obviously didn't have a mobile on it, so I suspected the mother also wouldn't. Wasn't too surprised that little girl didn't know the number of their landline either.

What are you gonna do? If something happens to that kid while in the store and you're the only present employee you're gonna have a bad time.

I sigh. "Hey girl, what's your name?"

"Tina."

"I'm Jason Reeves."

The little girl, happy like only kids can be if they think they did something smart or they knew something adds, "My surname is Dempers."

Now this rang a bell. I had a good customer with the same surname. It turns out that it's her dad. I didn't get paid enough to babysit. In fact I didn't even got paid enough to do my normal work so I call her dad at his workplace since we saved that number on our system.

"Hi Mr. Dempers, it's Jason from bookstore *xyz*."

"Oh hi Jason, how's it going?" he said pleasantly. "I don't remember having any open orders."

Yeah, erm . . . look, listen, do you have a daughter?"

If he wasn't confused before, he was now. "Yes, why do you ask?"

"What's her name?" (I just wanted to ensure it's really her dad and not just a stupid coincidence. If I think about it now, the little girl told me it's her dad so I don't know why I wasn't sure.)

After confirming it's his daughter the nice father apologizes for the Entitled Mother's behavior and tells me he's gonna pick his daughter up as soon as possible.

While waiting for him I picked up one of our sale-books (box with damaged books that we try to sell with huge discount before throwing away), a picture book from Disney. The little girl tries to read a little, I read a little. The father arrives quickly, his daughter breaking out in to a run to hug him, crying that mommy was mean to her. He soothes her and thanks me for babysitting her.

He gives me a bottle of wine and buys something small from the store. "If the mother shows up again, could you not tell her that I picked up my daughter?"

"What. Why?" I ask.

"If you don't feel like it you don't need to. Its rather complicated and you already did so much for us," he says before leaving.

In the evening the mother shows up. Just to point out—she dropped the little girl off here at about nine AM. It was now almost six in the evening. "Where's my daughter?"

Me, already having chugged about half the bottle of wine and thus a little boozed replied, "Your *what?*"

"My daughter," she repeated. "I dropped her in this store and you where here."

Admittedly I was way too drunk for work (but already decided to go for another job or homeless, both would have been better), so I repeated, "*Your what?*"

Now she was on the edge, and I did what I thought was the smartest thing to do. "A guy came into the store and picked her up. He seemed nice. Gave me some wine for her."

At this point I expected her to explode and attack me, but she just left the store.

A few weeks pass and the nice father and little girl come to the store, both happy to see me. He asks me if I got a few minutes. An excuse not to work? Obviously I took the time for . . . customer service so I gave the little girl the same book we read the last time and had a talk with her father.

The father and mother where in the middle of a divorce when she dropped Tina at our store. One of the reasons he wanted a divorce was that she "wasn't nice" to their daughter. Now in my country as a male it's rather hard to get custody for your child. No matter what. Tina wanted to be with her father but that doesn't matter so the mother dropping her in our store was a gift straight from the heavens.

That night the father took Tina to his sister overnight, while the mother pretended that Tina was sleeping at one of her friends. He wanted to call these friends "just to ensure that Tina is fine". Of course the mother didn't want that. Tina's friend didn't know where Tina was. The mother claimed she dropped Tina at the friend. So the father faked a panic and involved the police.

The mother insisted that Tina's friend kidnapped her. Police questioned the father and mother separately and the father told the police what happened. The mother still insisted on her dropping Tina at her friend. Father had proof of it being untrue since he already called the police when he dropped Tina at his sister's house.

In court the father apparently said something like "she can have all she wants, even my wine collection. I just want to be with my daughter."

The mother, knowing that daddy didn't have any money left and had some expensive wines, agreed. The daughter ended up with her father, while the mother paid alimony.

What the mother didn't know was that the father began replacing his wine collection before the divorce with the cheapest wines he could find at different discounters while gifting away the expensive ones. He knew that she was either gonna take everything from him or break his wine collection.

We both laughed about it, I gifted the book to Tina who seemed very happy. When the mother dropped her off she was shy, seemed small. Now she had such a big smile on her face and was curious about everything. She could read much better than a few weeks ago too. She seemed like a bird taking off to fly towards the sun. I absolutely hated my job, but situations like this make me a little bit nostalgic. Somehow I miss direct interactions with customers. On the other hand, I don't. I obviously don't.

12

You're a capable young man so I can grab whatever I want from your shopping cart

This happened around December of last year. My mum asked me to go grocery shopping because she was quite busy with something and I agreed to go so I went to Lidl.

I spent around ten minutes looking for things on the shopping list, and while there I decided to get a treat for myself because why not so I got some *Fin Carré* chocolate. I finally finished collecting everything and made my way to the till. I was standing in line while using my phone, just minding my business, when this overly loud parent with her very hyperactive kid who looked around eight came behind me in the line.

"You wouldn't mind letting us go in front of you, would you?" she asks.

I looked down in her cart which seemed to be a lot fuller than mine and I decided I'm not in a rush so why not and I replied, "Sure."

She thanked me and went on to go in front of me. My impression of this woman seemed normal, until the kid pointed at my cart. "Mum, look, it's that chocolate that you promised me to buy next time we go shopping."

"Oh yes darling I just remembered," she said before looking up to me. "May I grab the chocolate bar? The little one's been eager to get it."

Now this chocolate is somewhat far from the tills in this location so getting a new chocolate bar for myself would've been a chore. "I'm sorry I don't think I can give you the chocolate, it's quite far from the tills."

Her smile quickly turned into a death stare and she said in a loud voice, "Right, I don't care how far this chocolate is from here, someone like you is more than capable of getting a new bar so stop making George cross!"

"I don't care how capable I am," I replied. "I'm not going anywhere and this chocolate is staying in the cart."

There was a lot going through my head at this point but I remember how the kid was reaching inside my cart and trying to grab the chocolate so I quickly grabbed it myself and held it in my hand.

"Mum the guy took the chocolate!" he wailed.

"Right I've had enough." The mother reached for my hand to grab the chocolate, but I moved away in time and decided to go directly to the cashier and ask him to call a manager. The cashier seemed to have witnessed everything and so he informed the manager about what happened. No more than two minutes of me awkwardly standing and the manager arrives.

She walks up to the Entitled Mother and quietly asks her to leave while the mother kept trying to incriminate me somehow until she finally paid for her groceries and left. The cashier, the manager and I all had a laugh about it after she left.

Now that I think about it, that scene wasn't worth a chocolate bar but oh well.

13

Posted by **SocietalMember**

You WILL date my daughter, or I'll get you FIRED!

I'm a seventeen year old male and work at a Segway tour company. It's actually really fun—I get to ride Segways around the city, talk to people and get paid to do it! Plus the tipping isn't bad.

There was a tour booked a couple of days ago and I came in about twenty minutes early to answer emails and get everything ready. The group shows up, mother and daughter, and that's when things get interesting.

I check them in and give them the standard paperwork. "Alright I have some waivers for you to sign. How old are you?"

"Uh, sixteen," the daughter replies.

"Ok, then you don't need to sign a waiver." I ask this because if kids are younger than eighteen their parents sign the waivers for them, but the Entitled Parent only heard me say the first part, not about not needing to sign a waiver, so she thought I was just asking her daughter how old she was. This was probably what started it all.

We go on the tour, and while I'm giving my spiel the Entitled Parent keeps interrupting me to tell me stuff about her daughter almost as if to find if we are compatible.

". . . So this non-profit organization opened in—"

"Are you in college?" the mother asks.

I laugh. "No, I'm a junior in high school." I'm usually pretty free with info about myself on tours because it helps keep people relaxed and initiates conversations during lulls in the tour. Plus it helps with tipping.

"Oh, my daughter is also a junior. She is an artist."

Stuff like this keeps happening throughout the tour, and every time the poor daughter gets redder and redder. My mom does this too where she just tells random mall attendants about me, so I know what this girl is going through and feel her pain.

At the end of the tour I tell the two of them that they have fifteen minutes to go around the town and then they can meet me back at the Segway place. I get back and start getting things set up for their return. They roll in (pardon the pun) and I take their Segways to start charging them.

"So what do you think of my daughter?" the mother asks suddenly.

"Pardon me, what?"

"I saw you checking her out during the tour. Are you gonna ask her out?"

"Mom, stop!" the daughter moans.

"Um, ma'am I just recently got out of a relationship and I'm really not looking for anything right now."

"What?" she sputters. "Is my daughter not good enough for you?"

"No, that's not it," I say in a rush, "I just said that I just got out of a relations—"

"—You are going to date my daughter and that's final!"

"You can't tell me what to do! I'm not your kid, and if I don't want to date your daughter I don't have to! Besides, you haven't even asked her if she wants to date me!"

"Yeah, I don't want to date him," the daughter added.

"See!"

"I'm going to call your boss and tell him about your terrible customer service!" the mother yells. "You're never going to work in this city again!"

I pulled out my phone. "Alright, you want to call him and explain this situation? How you're trying to force me to date your daughter and get me fired for saying no?"

I guess the absurdity of the situation finally sunk in because her face transitioned from pure rage to slight confusion. "Wait, maybe I don't want to—"

"No, let's call him." I start to go through my contacts and press my boss's name. "Let's have this conversation."

"I don't think that's a good idea . . ." she says as the phone starts ringing, then looks at her daughter. "Let's go!"

The mother then runs out the door. After a moment the daughter turns to me and says "I'm sorry" before she follows her mom.

I hang up the phone before my boss answers and start cleaning the Segways.

14

Posted by **Cakeikins**

EK steals my wet towel turban and EM freaks out when she realises I'm a social worker.

This happened about five years ago when I was working as a newly qualified social worker (I know, lynch mob me, I don't anymore it was a nightmare).

It was a rough morning and I had spit and vomit on me. As standard practice I kept a spare set of court clothes in my car so I had something to change into. I felt pretty disgusting and wanted a shower so I took an early lunch and went to my gym nearby the office to shower and change.

I came out of the shower and put my hair up into a towel turban before walking back to the lockers. The changing area was empty except for one kid, a boy about eight or nine. A bit weird for him to be alone, but I assumed his mum must've been in the only occupied stall so I didn't think too much of it. I smiled to acknowledge him and got to my locker to grab my things to change into.

The boy looked at me, pointed at my towel turban and said, "What's that?"

"Oh it's a towel turban. Pretty neat huh? It stays up better than a regular towel."

"Cool," he replied, and started to reach for my head.

"Excuse me, what are you doing?" I asked.

"I just want to see it."

"Err, no. I'm using it, sorry."

At this point in my life, I'm pretty used to kids being a bit inappropriate and it's my job to make sure they understand but I wasn't expecting it here. He looked a bit pissed, but went back to what was probably his mum's phone.

I dress quickly and get my things to go over to the mirror and take the turban off to dry my hair. I'm flipping my hair around and I notice that this kid comes up to the mirror, then leaves again.

Again I think nothing of it and finish drying my hair, turn the hairdryer off, reach for my turban . . . and it's not there.

I know what he's done and I whip around and look at him. He's turning a shade of red but staring fixedly on his phone so as to ignore me.

I'm trying to remain calm, but I've been spat at, vomited on and now someone has stolen my towel turban in a single day? I walk back over and do my best *I've had enough of this bullshittery* voice. "Please return the turban. Now."

He keeps ignoring me, so I repeat myself. "Please return the turban. Now."

He's gone a deep shade of red, refuses to look at me and mumbles something like *I didn't take it*.

I've had it at this point, so go over to the only occupied stall and knock on the door. "Excuse me, is this your son out here?"

The Entitled Mother opens the door and looks at me, thoroughly annoyed. "What?"

"Is this your son? He has taken my towel turban, I have asked for it back but he is not returning it. Please ask him to hand it back and I won't inform the gym's staff."

"What the fuck is a towel turban?" she asks.

I start to explain, but the kid butts in. "It's a hair towel that stays up better than a normal towel!"

We both look at him, and she says, "Ok . . . so what do you want?"

"I want my towel turban back please."

"He wouldn't just take something. You obviously just lost it. You shouldn't go around accusing people because you lose things!"

I'm getting annoyed. "Well, he will have no problem emptying his bag then. If he has it, he can just hand it back and if I'm mistaken I will apologize."

She looks at the kid and it's obvious that he's lying, except to her apparently. "Don't be fucking stupid. I'm not letting you rummage through his things like he's some kind of thief! Look at you, you are harassing a little boy in a changing room!"

I inhale to try and stop my eyes doing a three sixty degree roll. "I'm not asking to touch anything. I'm asking for you to go through his bag for my turban. That is all. If you are not willing, I will go to the staff and ask them to sort this out." (I know it's just a freaking towel turban, but theft is theft. It's also pink and cute so I'm not letting anyone have it).

"So you're threatening me now?"

I know a circular argument when I hear one so I go to the door, lean out and call for someone to come and sort it out.

Enter gym trainer dude. "What's going on?"

He looks between the three of us. The kid has gone back to staring a hole through the phone so the mother positions herself between the trainer and her son. "This crazy bitch is harassing my son and trying to go through his bag! She needs throwing out! She—"

"—That isn't what happened," I say quickly. "Her son has taken my towel turban, and I would like it returned."

I just keep looking at this kid, and trainer looks down at him too. "Ok, so what happened mate? Did you take the towel?"

The kid mumbles something about how I must've lost it and the mother jumps in. "See? He didn't take it. He's so traumatized he can barely say anything!" She then bends down to him and hugs him saying "it'll be alright" and she "won't let me get away with this". Very dramatic.

I turn to the trainer and explain the whole event.

"Ok, so, why don't we just check his bag?" he asks.

The kid then starts wailing and the Entitled Mother begins ranting about how this is harassment.

The trainer looks uncomfortable. "That's literally the only way I think I can solve this."

The mother stands up and tries to push past me, but I'm not moving and the room is small so she fails. She then starts swearing and thrusts the kids backpack at the trainer. "Fine! Check it! He hasn't taken it, and when you don't find it I want her thrown out and for you to apologize and get the manager!"

The kid begins to wail.

The trainer obviously finds the pink, wet turban towel in the bag. He picks it up and kind of just looks at it. The kid wails even more and *tries to grab it,* but the trainer holds it out of his reach. "Right. So . . . so . . . this is yours?"

"Yes," I reply, "thank you."

I stuff the "coveted" turban towel into my bag and get out my cars keys and I.D. lanyard. As I put the lanyard over my head something audibly clicked in EM's head—that's a social worker ID.

She yanks the kid's arm, snatches the bag from the trainer and I move to let her pass. The trainer looks super confused and I explain that she must've just been embarrassed that her son stole my turban. But I knew she was panicking because she realized what my job was and that her son was out of school stealing pink wet turban towels.

15

Posted by **Echinoderm only**

At two days past my due date, I shouldn't have used the 'expectant mothers/parents with small children' parking spot.

My pregnancy was okay up until the last month. It was ninety five degrees outside, I was retaining so much water that my sandals hardly fit on the biggest setting and I was constantly in pain. It sucked.

I waddle to the store for a couple last minute things for baby, and I was so relieved that there was a parking spot for preggo's & parents near the entrance. I pulled in and took a few moments to chug water and gather my things when I notice a car pull up to my left. They were half in the handicap parking stall and yelling something out the window.

I rolled my window down and hear "You shouldn't be in that spot if you don't have kids. My son shouldn't have to walk from the back of the parking lot" or something to that effect.

I was a little stunned to be yelled at, but calmly told her that I was *very* pregnant and this stall was for pregnant women too.

She kept talking to her son, but *at me,* you know what I mean? "Sorry son, you have to walk in the heat because this lady parked in our spot."

I opened my door and hoisted my giant, land-whale-esque body out of my car. She was still turned around "talking to her son" and when she finally saw me, I was about three feet away from her window.

I bent down (no, I tilted my head down.) "Do you see how pregnant I am? I think you and your son will be okay walking."

I saw the son then and he was like seven years old. The kid can walk. She just sighed and drove away.

I was so pissed. I wish I said more to her.

16

Girl I babysit has a weak immune system, EP tries to get her unvaxxed kid to take her mask/hug/sneeze on her.

I "babysit" this girl who we will call Emily. She is by far the sweetest girl in existence and even though I call it "babysitting" I have stopped charging her mother and just come over and hang-out with her for the most part (her mom still calls it babysitting because Emily is eight and I am twenty three).

I use to work with her mom at a coffee-shop and that's when I learned about Emily's story. She was born with some sort of compromised immune system. I don't know the full details or what it's called but I know that she has grown up most of her life in her house. She can't go to a normal school (has a private teacher person though) and can't really play with kids her own age. Her mom is a single mom and one day for work she had to bring her daughter in because her normal babysitter cancelled last minute. I was actually finishing my shift so I offered to bring her to my place (it was close by) and keep her safe from germs and stuff.

Since then we've hit it off on the universal tool of love and connecting with kids, Pokémon and I have gone over to her place to hang out with her ever since. I do get a full on disinfection bath when I hang with her. She's gotten a bit better though as before I had to wear almost a sanitary suit but now just a good hand washing and some special spray stuff.

Admittedly a bit overboard but Emily's mom is super protective and loving because to my knowledge she is the only family she has left.

They live in an apartment with no patio or condo park and I was hanging out with Emily one evening playing Pokémon when I noticed she was looking outside a lot. She'd never experienced snow before and her favorite Pokémon is Glaceon, an ice type.

I started scheming and came up with a solution for her to enjoy the snow. I presented the idea to her Mom about going to an untouched spot of snow. We live near a few dog parks that also serve as nature preservation spots and I knew of a spot that dogs don't go down and there was a bunch of untouched snow. It's not too remote as it's near some houses but it's got a bunch of trees surrounding it.

I pulled out my full out anti-germ snowsuit idea using duck tape to seal gaps and using my snowboard goggles to protect her face and keep her mask on tightly. She loved the idea and agreed as long as we went during the day when there are less people around because they are at work or school. We told Emily the idea and this sweet girl started crying with so much joy.

The day came that we were going out and she could not keep her excitement in. We disinfected everything—I got my anti-germ belt (spare masks, sanitizer, other anti-germ stuff) and put it all on her. Everything was a bit too big on her and she had an awkward time walking but she was still having lots of fun. I put us under the germ-field (it's an umbrella with plastic all the way around that goes down to the ground) and we made it to the untouched spot.

We had such a blast making snowmen (more like snow-Pokémon as she really wanted to try and make a Glaceon out of snow), snow angels and so on. Everything was great until I heard a sudden "Excuse me!" and see the Entitled Parent and her boy coming towards us. My mothering instinct came out and I had Emily stand behind me. "Hello. Is there something I can help you with?"

"I was hoping my son could come play with your daughter," the mother said. "He's sick and had to stay home from school today and he saw you two playing. That's okay right?"

Nope, nope, nope, nope, *big nope!* Keep that child away from my girl! Also I didn't want to bother correcting her on the daughter thing as if you did meet us we would seem like a mother and daughter. "Sorry we're just having an 'us' play date. Also if your son is sick shouldn't he be resting?"

Her son looked like he was dying—sluggish, coughing, sneezing and white as the snow.

"My son will be fine, he just needs to work off the illness." She then almost pushes her son towards Emily and we back up.

"Emily here can get sick very easily and I just want to protect her." As I'm replying Emily gives me that look of *I don't want to get sick and die let's leave.* "If you want to play here we will be on our way then."

"Why does she get sick easily?" the mother asks. "Is she vaccinated?"

"Yes she is."

"That's why, the vaccines probably ruined her system! Shame on you for putting your daughter through that. She's going to get autism! My boy is healthy and vaccine free!"

Nope, nope, nope, nope, nope! "And on that note we're leaving now."

"You should be letting her get sick!" she insists. "That's how they become strong!"

"I want your mask!" the kid yells. "It's a Pikachu right? I want it, I want it, I want it, I want it, I want it!"

"How much for the mask?" the mother asks.

"It's not for sale," I reply. "You can get plenty online and probably a much cheaper one than this."

The mother balks. "Just give us the mask! Timmy go get the mask."

The boy runs over to Emily, literally reaching for the mask. I step in front of him and gently push him away but this boy was so sick he sneezed and got snot all over me. I immediately start disinfecting and the mom just scoffs. "Look how ridiculous you are! Let my son make your daughter sick!"

We're trying to walk away but as I mentioned Emily's suit limits her mobility and because I just got sneezed on I can't pick her up now without risking her getting sick. The mother catches up, grabs Emily's arm and the son gets in closer.

Admittedly I don't quite remember the next part as I just saw red. All I know was the Entitled Parent was on the ground, her son was crying and I had Emily in my arms.

"I'm sorry, (I'm Canadian) but you can't just—"

"—*how dare you!*" she screeches. "I am calling the police. You probably abuse your daughter."

Emily, being the smartest girl in the whole gosh darn cute-iverse, jumps to my defense. "And I will tell the police you attempted to kidnap me and stab Gobityn!"

I looked down at the mother and saw she had pulled out what looks to be one of those mini switchblades you put on your keychain.

The mother just grabbed her son and left.

I brought Emily home and we had a big disinfectant party. I told her mom what had happened and apologized to the point I lost my voice. Thank Arceus that Emily did not get sick. And despite what had happen she still says it was the best day of her life.

I did ask Emily what had happened when I started seeing red. She said she didn't quite remember herself other then I stormed forward and grabbed her up. The Entitled Parent tried lunging towards me and I punched her. The boy got scared and started crying, then the mother started yelling and pulled out the blade and I kicked her away. I seriously doubt this happened but she said I was a superhero and whatever I did clearly stopped the situation and potentially saved Emily's life.

I went through my coat jacket a few days later and found a wallet in my coat. It was clearly a kid's wallet. I didn't recognize it as one of Emily's so I looked inside and saw "If lost return to *Entitled Parent's* house address" but I didn't realize it was the Entitled Parent's son so I went to the house to return it.

Entitled Parent opens the door.

After a moment of silence I handed over the wallet and she burst into tears. I tried calming her down and got a bit more information.

Apparently I got the wallet when the kid dropped it. I went to pick it up and she shoved me away so I must've just auto-pilot put it in my jacket.

Her son was sicker then she realized and was in the hospital in critical condition. She became terrified of the idea that she got Emily sick and also potentially sentenced someone to death but was relieved to hear that she was okay.

The mother wasn't sure what happened with her son so me being the damn sucker that I am I decided to help her google more information. It was some sort of flu and *it's preventable with vaccines.*

She also explained she hasn't been thinking straight because she is pregnant and having hormone issues. I talked with her for a while and strongly encouraged her getting vaccines for both her children. I gave her my number if she wanted to talk more about it. She did call to let me know that the son is making a recovery.

17

Posted by **CharlottesSpooks**

EM tries to send me away from my mother's party because my lazy eye scares her daughter.

When I was small I was in a car accident which damaged my eyesight and the look of my eye itself. It's not really a lazy eye as my pupil just lazily rolls around my eye most of the time. Some nerve thing, doctors say.

My mother hosted a great party with grills and everything and invited all her friends from the neighborhood. Innocent, right? Well . . . not really.

So I was eating with my friend when a little kid comes to our table. She was a cute little girl that said she was lost so I lowered myself to her level to ask about her mom to find her. As I did she ran off crying.

I shrugged it off. There was a lot of parents that are more experienced, but this is where the fun begins.

The Entitled Mother and her daughter approached me when I was taking another burger that my mom made. She took a look at me and then made an obviously disgusted sound. "What is that?"

"What is what, ma'am?" I asked.

"What's with your eye? No wonder it made my daughter cry!"

"Wha—"

"—Can't you at least hold it up?" she asks rudely.

"Do I look like I can?" I muttered.

"Don't raise your voice, young lady! You do not belong to this party anyway."

"Why?" I ask incredulously.

"You scare kids!"

At this time people hear us and my mom storms in, furious. She explained everything and sends the entitled parent away, the Entitled Mother swearing at my mom before going off.

I love my mom.

18

Posted by **Murgeruni**

Little Entitled Crap Eats Crab In Aquarium Store And Mom Defends Him.

I work at a mom and pop pet store in the eastern United States, and while my expertise is in aquatics I try to be a jack of all trades. The day that this happened was rather uneventful, at least until the Entitled Mother and her kid entered the store.

My store was pretty modest so it was fairly easy to see customers come in and out, especially in the fish department, so I got the first look at these magnificent creatures entering the shop. A forty something woman talking on her cell, her hair obviously dyed blond and outfit practically screaming *midlife crisis* while her child was in tow. The kid must have been seven or eight, glued to his Switch, his shirt covered in what looked like a mixture of pizza sauce, soda and plenty of mystery stains.

At first things were pretty normal, the kid not caring about anything in the store while the mother was getting enraged at him for not paying attention, though that changed rather quickly. They were near the ferrets when she took the kids switch, immediately causing a reaction of screaming and pouting before being distracted by some of the fish over in my department.

The way my store's fish department is set up two fifth's of it is freshwater, two fifth's is equipment and the rest is saltwater. Given we weren't really known for saltwater we only kept pretty generic yet sought after fish like hippo tangs, various clownfish, six-line wrasses, etc. The thing about the first two is because of Finding Nemo kids are always drawn to the "Dorys" or "Nemos".

The first thing the kid did was head over to the small assortment of hippo tangs we had, practically pressing his dirty face against the glass as he yelled out "Dory!" as loud as he could.

The mother hailed me down from algae scrubbing and this started the encounter. I like to act casual around the workplace as I find it lowers any sort of anxiety a customer has and makes me way more approachable. "Hey there, how's your night going? Need help with something?"

The mother rolled her eyes before pointing to the tang and demanding a price rather rudely. "How much for this thing?"

After shifting gears from a casual standing to a more professional one I simply told her that the tang was a hundred and sixty dollars as he was a good size tang. Of course she scoffed but what came next was a bit more worrying.

She pulled out thirty dollars from her purse and placed it on the desk we use to bag fish. "That's all you're getting. Bag him."

Things start to go poorly from here.

It's worth noting that it was quarter past nine at this point, the store having closed fifteen minutes ago, though we make it a policy not to ask customers to leave until nine thirty. It was just my manager and myself at this point, my manager in the office closing down registers, so essentially it was like I was the only employee in the store.

Seeing the woman placing the thirty dollars on the table I raised an eyebrow before leaning against the wall. "Do you have a saltwater tank?"

She didn't take this well, screaming without a second passing. "None of your fucking business, now bag my fish you cocky little shit."

I simply refused and slid her money back towards her before she slid it back, now more pissed off.

"I'm going to get your ass fired if you don't bag my fish right now!"

The kid was getting pissed at the interaction, screaming like a banshee about how he wanted the tang, still referring to it as Dory, and beginning to stomp his feet in a tantrum. Soon enough I was asking them to leave.

This is where I fucked up.

I should have called the cops knowing that she wasn't going to leave without a fight. The kid was on the floor at this point, pounding his fists on the floor as snot dripped down his face while the mother tried to guilt me.

"Sorry sweetie, this guy doesn't want you to have the fish. He's perfectly fine with you having no fish friend to make you happy." She then turned back to me. "Do you see what you did, you stupid fuck? You are breaking my angel's heart because you're being too much of a Jew to sell me the fish."

Internally I was laughing. This kind of situation happened now and again, but the anti-Semitism was a new one. I had figured everything was starting to resolve at this point. I was mistaken.

The kid *flipped his shit.*

You know how some opera singers can break glass with their voice?

This kid would have a knack for something like that. He was screaming as loud as humanly possible while managing to reach into the tank. At last my manager had made his way out of the office and was watching what was going on. The Entitled Kid grabbed a piece of live rock, accidentally grabbing a long spine urchin.

Angry screaming turned to wails of pain as he pulled the rock out of the tank, a poor little pompom crab in tow. At this point I was less focused on the kid and more focused on making sure my manager was calling 911, which he did. When I turned around I saw something that still gives me nightmares to this day.

The kid had been clutching his hand while his mother tried to help him, something hanging out of his mouth. The poor little pompom crab had been crushed by the kid, then he shoved it in his mouth and chomped down on—leaving a little claw hanging out of his mouth.

The next two minutes was a strange combination of astonishment and panic, me telling the kid not to move his hand since he would break the spines of the urchin while the mother began hitting me with her crappy purse screaming that I hurt her kid.

"Your kid shoved his hand in to a tank, one with toxic animals nonetheless and did this to himself. Calm the fuck down and leave him alone so when the paramedics get here they can get the spines out."

"How dare you," she screams. "You expect me to let my angel suffer? If you just sold me the stupid fish this would have never happened!"

"Your kid reached into the tank and ate a crab, what the fuck did you teach this kid?"

"Don't you ever, ever tell me how to raise my angel! *He had the right* to eat that crab. You took something from him and he took something from you."

By the end of this interaction the paramedics had arrived, restraining the kid and taking him into an ambulance as the police tried to sort things out.

Unsurprisingly the mother tried to pin everything on me, saying I threw and urchin at him (really?) and he ate the crab in a panic. Equally unsurprisingly we had the entire thing on CCTV, including the woman hitting me with her purse.

She was arrested for aggravated assault as apparently she had stuffed the rock into her bag to give it that extra punch. I didn't notice until after the paramedics told me that I was bleeding on my leg from the jagged live rock.

After getting a statement the cops left, the mother and son going off to where ever the hell the cops took them and I got out of everything with eight stitches and a three hundred bonus from my boss for handling the situation without anyone getting seriously injured.

Later I heard the kid had actually got stung by a fox face's dorsal spines and that sent him into a blind rage. The mom got a plea deal and she ended up with a huge fine, some jail time and some other shit.

This was by far the worst situation I had ever had in the store and I still can't believe the outcome till this day. This was three years ago.

I was at work the other day when I saw a kid pouting over a mom not let him get a hippo tang and this has been brought to the front of my mind ever since.

I had sat down with my boss this morning and asked about the events and while I didn't get all the answers I was looking for, this is what he had to say. As I've stated, I still stay up now and again wondering what could make people act this way and I did get a few answers. According to my boss, the woman was the wife of a known meth dealer, which didn't exactly surprise me given what happens in my town.

The cops never had gotten a warrant to search their property for whatever reason, but this had given them the opportunity. From what he was told the woman was abusing prescription anti-depressants and drugs for Attention Deficit Disorder and had a meltdown. Although I pressed charges I never was called to court and from what we could assume she most likely struck a deal with the police to rat out her husband. I don't know the story with the kid, though it wouldn't surprise me if he was on the same toxic cocktail of drugs. In regards to the CCTV footage, he had told me that he handed it over to the police and couldn't show me for "legal reasons" but that there wasn't much to see other than my manager running to the sales floor. The way our CCTV cams are placed only really show part of the sales floor, the office, and the register counter.

Medical bills was way easier, I have been on an expensive med not covered by most insurances for most of my life so I've always had to pay out the ass for a really good insurance company and this time it paid off. I ended up with a hundred dollar charge for the ambulance, though my boss reimbursed me.

Honestly this was just a really surreal situation and it had really confused me for a while, but I'm pretty happy I got things cleared up and hopefully the kid is now getting the love and direction he should have been getting all along.

19

"You Can't Name Your Baby That"

This one happened to my mom when she was pregnant with me.

Back in the late nineties when Sears wasn't sad and dying my mother was their assistant manager. Her boss was also pregnant and this generally wasn't an issue, until the day it became one.

My parents spent a long time choosing baby names, and when I turned out to be a girl they really wanted my name to be gender neutral to prevent future trouble finding jobs (yes, that is the actual reason). My middle name remained the same as when they thought I was a boy - Ryan. When they decided on my full name my mom told her friends about it and one of them ended up telling the manager.

As my mother was on lunch-break this lady storms in, already red and furious. "I heard you were naming your baby Ryan."

My mother is of course stunned and stays silent for a few moments before finally answering. "That's her middle name, yes?"

"Your baby is a girl!" The woman exclaims, as though this is some sort of great revelation.

My mother nods.

The woman snaps, growing redder in the process. "Ryan is a boy's name."

"Actually it's gender neutral." At this point, my mother's surprise is wearing off and growing into a bit of righteous confusion. "Is there a problem with the name?"

"You can't name your baby that." The woman is practically shouting at this point, "I'm naming my son that!"

My mother stares at her, trying to work out what kind of mental gymnastics it takes to decide your choice of baby name should give you the authority to veto someone else's baby name.

"So?" she finally asks.

"Change your baby's middle name or I'm going to fire you," The woman says, drawing a crowd with this whole scene to witness the utter insanity that was her outburst. People who could act as witnesses for my mother if she attempted such a thing.

"I don't think you can do that." My mother answers flatly.

She couldn't even fire my mother on some other infraction because there was no other infraction - the staff was friendly with my mother and she had brought up sales in her area by a lot.

The woman stops for a moment, maybe realizing that my mother was right on that point and once again becomes demanding. "Change your baby's middle name! I chose Ryan fist!"

Ah yes, calling dibs. Surely my mother would have to respect a grown woman calling dibs on a very common name.

"Ryan is my maiden name." My mom answers flatly.

At this, the woman stops, still furious, sputters for a moment and finally stomps off.

My middle name is Ryan. My mother's boss named her son Dylan instead.

20

Maleficient's Revenge: How my cousin exacted revenge for YEARS of EP behavior

My mom is the oldest of four children and gave birth to me a few months before her youngest sister (let's call her Cruella) gave birth to my cousin (Maleficient). From the day she brought Maleficient home Cruella groomed my cousin to be a beauty pageant kid.

She started getting Maleficient's hair done as soon as she could and raised Maleficient to only wear dresses and very dainty shoes. When I briefly lived with my aunt she used the money my mom sent home to provide for my care to get Maleficient new clothes and her hair done. Cruella had a full-time job as a grocery store cashier and also received child support from Maleficient's father, who was in the U.S. Air Force, but she spent thousands of dollars on making sure her daughter was always beauty pageant ready.

When we got older I was a grade level ahead of Maleficient. Cruella made Maleficient compete with me academically regardless of the difference in our classes. We were both good students and lived in different states, but Cruella would call my mom once a month and would ask detailed questions about my report cards. If Mom told her that I earned all A's, Cruella would implement various punishments until Maleficient had just as good or better grades.

At first Cruella would belittle her own daughter with taunts. Then she would deny buying Maleficient any cookies, toys, and more until her grades "improved". When we started hitting our growth spurts Cruella would then make Maleficient wear old dresses and shoes that were way too small as punishment.

Naturally this made life difficult for my mom and me. Maleficient grew to resent me and she often did petty things to get me into trouble like breaking my grandma's doll collection, breaking dishes and even fought me a couple of times when I refused to be bullied. My mom stopped discussing my grades with Cruella, which worked until Mom and I moved back to her hometown (where Cruella lived) and enrolled in the same school as

Maleficient.

Then Cruella began to "volunteer" at the school on report card days just to find out what Maleficient's and my grades were. This continued into our college years.

I ended up dropping out of college after three semesters as I had developed a drinking problem. I had to undergo a few months of treatment. Maleficient was enrolled in college by this time, and Cruella maintained her streak of competition by calling my mom to report how well my cousin was doing before snidely pointing out that I was no longer in college.

I changed phone numbers after Cruella called me one day to tell me that Maleficient was applying for study abroad and then asked how my "borderline minimum wage" retail job was going. The irony was that Maleficient would end up being a fourth year junior in college when I finally returned to college.

By the time I returned to college our grandma (Mom and Cruella's mom) was in a nursing home due to dementia-related issues. She had been diagnosed while we were in high school but the disease was progressing rapidly. Mom, being the eldest child, quit her job to spend every day at the nursing home talking to grandma, reading to grandma and everything else. Mom wanted to have grandma returned to grandma's home, but Cruella refused.

Cruella had secured power of executor of the estate shortly after grandma's diagnosis, meaning that she had the ability to place Grandma in the home despite her siblings' protests. It also meant that Cruella technically had ownership of Grandma's home and the land on which it resided.

Fast forward a couple of years – Maleficient had begun dating a local pastor's son (let's call him Charming) and they got engaged in April after dating for three months. Cruella, coincidentally, was good friends of Charming's mother. She wasted no time in bragging to my mom how Maleficient was engaged to be married. At this time I was graduating from college, which really got under Cruella's skin. I still didn't talk directly to her but I did keep up communication with my cousin.

When I talked to her about the upcoming nuptials Maleficient revealed that Cruella was planning to take Grandma off life support and would use the money from Grandma's estate and insurance to pay for a lavish wedding. Maleficient also revealed that she did not want to marry

Charming, was fed up with college (she was a seventh year senior) and was basically living the life Cruella had created for her.

I mentioned to my mom what Maleficient had said about taking Grandma off life support, and Mom was livid. She called Maleficient and they crafted the revenge together.

In June, Cruella decided to host a very over the top party to celebrate the engagement. Mom and I chose not to attend and went to visit Grandma in the hospital together that night. So Maleficient's actions were reported to me by Maleficient herself, but I'm going to paraphrase them.

Cruella had organized the evening so that the parents of the engaged couple and the engaged couple could stand to tell everyone in the room how amazing their respective families were. Charming and his parents had already gushed their praises for Cruella, and it was Maleficient's turn. Maleficient thanked Cruella for raising her, thanked Charming's parents for raising such a good son . . . *then announced that the wedding was off.*

She took the opportunity to tell Charming that she did care about him but would not marry him just because it was what their families expected from *soon to be parents.* Maleficient then left the party and spent the night with one of her friends from high school.

This humiliated Cruella on a personal and financial level. She had already paid non-refundable deposits for a caterer, wedding reception hall, dress and limo among many more. All out of pocket. Furthermore, Cruella and Charming's parents were very against premarital sex which made Maleficient's unexpected announcement even more appalling.

Cruella had planned to keep the pregnancy as hidden as possible with the dress she had selected and Maleficient was expected to remain complicit. She called Maleficient and raged at her several times, but Maleficient stood her ground. She returned the car Cruella had bought for her and informed Cruella that she was dropping out of college as well, which would leave Cruella *thousands of dollars* in debt on student loans.

Their drama took a back seat when Grandma passed away in early August. Maleficient had gotten a job in a corporate office by then, and showed up to the funeral looking very happy and very pregnant. After the funeral we had a reception and Cruella called Mom, me, Maleficient and my uncle and other aunt into a room together to announce that she was going to sell Grandma's house and land and would split up Grandma's life insurance policy money as she saw fit.

It was the expected announcement from her and of course she phrased it like this was what Grandma would have wanted.

I don't know who was smiling wider between my mom or Maleficient when they announced that they were contesting her power as executor of the estate. As Grandma's diagnosis of dementia had been announced just days before Cruella secured her position my mom had consulted a lawyer to contest the decisions Cruella had made.

Mom and Cruella ended up going to court and the matter was resolved less than a year later—Cruella's position as executor of the estate was overruled due to Grandma's mental capacity at the time. This meant that, outside of a life insurance policy Cruella had taken on Grandma, she received no money directly. Maleficient is paying off her student loans but Cruella is still paying other debts from living beyond her means.

Mom agreed to let Maleficient and her daughter move into Grandma's old house, and she and Charming are co-parenting.

My cousin really appreciated the comments and feedback this post got and was really, really happy that so many people were supportive of her ordeal. Thank you everyone for your thoughts.

21

Posted by **Kibufox**

Entitled mom ends up in court.

Let me preface this by saying that this happened a very long time ago, and while I could come to a reasonable approximation of the dialogue that surrounded this I won't bother. I don't recall everything that was said, just some of the circumstances.

First off I am a model railroader. Specifically, I model in O scale. For reference that means that the average locomotive is about three to four inches tall, and up to a foot long (depending on type that is).

One summer I was taking part in a model railroad fair at our local mall where I was displaying some of my models. Being that I'm from the United States the fact that I modeled the British Isles (GWR for you Brit readers) meant that my display really stood out. Now, as there's always kids at these types of shows I had taken to putting a Plexiglas side around my layout to prevent children from reaching in and touching things or damaging various parts of the structures and models that went with the railroad.

While I was watching one locomotive I had just received leave the staging area (it's a small three track system that lets me funnel trains into the layout and then out as needed) I remembered this one lady making comments about the "cute little trains". Getting that train running at a nice but slow pace I approached her and smiled, asking if she had any questions.

The lady never missed a beat, pointing to the train I had just started and told me that her son liked trains and I should sell her one for him. Now, truth be told, this wasn't an uncommon thing to happen. People (usually other modelers) may ask if some units are up for sale. Sometimes they are, but typically not. I explained to her that the locomotive wasn't for sale, and that even if it was she wouldn't have liked the price anyway - noting that the engine she was pointing to had cost me close to a thousand dollars.

The lady was having none of it, offering me ten dollars for it since it was *obviously* a toy.

I ignored her and went back to getting the next train set up on the staging track, waiting for that one to return. As I do this I hear an odd sound and look up just in time to see the lady picking the locomotive up off the track and moving to hand it to her kid. I called out for her to stop, which may have been a mistake, because she promptly dropped it on the ground.

The engine, though somewhat robust and heavy, was made of rather soft brass. When it hit the ground there was a sickening crunch. I knew from the sound that the engine was done for. Broken beyond repair.

The lady just looked down at it, shrugged, and kicked it back under the table before starting to walk off. Thankfully, security quickly caught up and detained her while police were called. All the while she kept saying 'it's just a toy, men don't play with toys', while ignoring the fact she was surrounded by dozens of train layouts, with just as many grown men showing off their work.

Police arrested her on destruction of private property charges, while the mall itself barred her from ever setting foot on their property again. Later, with her information on hand from the police report, I filed a case against her for the replacement of the locomotive.

You won't believe it, but she had the gall to try to convince the judge that it was just a toy, and the receipts I had for purchase of the locomotive weren't real. Saying that she had seen the exact same locomotive at Wal-Mart herself. Well, the case ended up in my favor with her having to pay me replacement costs, as well as some punitive damages. The judge ended the case with the warning that "just because you want something, doesn't give you the right to simply take it".

From the criminal side of things, I think the lady ended up with forty or so hours of community service and a substantial fine as well.

Here's hoping she learned her lesson.

22

Posted by **BigusSpekus**

I do not care if you have Cancer, my child DESERVES your seat!

This encounter happened about seven months ago. The kid was very polite and sorry, so this story isn't about him. Also, I'm translating this into English so bear with me.

About a year ago I was diagnosed with cancer of the nasal cavity (stage 2). The tumor was quite large, but thankfully it did not spread into other tissues, thus it was still "contained". To get it removed I had to undergo aggressive chemotherapy to make it smaller. Thanks to the chemo, I had severe alopecia (hair loss), which made most of my hair and even eyebrows and eyelashes fall out. At some point I went bald, but I wore a wig, because I didn't want to look like a skinhead/Neo-Nazi (I'm six foot four and pretty muscular, so I thought people would assume).

After a long chemo session in the hospital I took the bus home one day. There's only one bus that goes from the hospital to where I live, so I took that one only to see it was absolutely packed. I felt like shit thanks to the chemo, so I asked a middle aged dude to let me sit. He was very understanding and gave me his spot without complaining (if you're reading this, thanks bro).

Two stops later, enter the Entitled Parent, a lovely whale with an "I demand a parley with the CEO" haircut and a twelve or so year old kid. It took her roughly five seconds to see the bus was packed, start looking for a free seat, spot me and start marching (or, in her case, trying to fit in the aisle between the seats while shoving others aside) to me.

When I saw her, I knew I was screwed.

"Hey, could you let my kid sit down?" she asked once she was standing next to me.

"You mean me?"

"Who else?"

"Oh, I'm sorry," I reply, "but I'm on my way from the hospital and—"

"—So are we. (Nonsense, the stop was a few kilometers away from the hospital.) My boy just broke his leg and we're coming straight from the ER".

Her kid was standing next to her, without any support and clearly embarrassed. "He's standing next to you completely fine."

"Look here, *boy* (I am twenty one), my kid *deserves* to sit down."

"Look madam, I'm sorry but I just got back from a chemo session in the hospital and I need to sit down and rest," I said, moving my wig a bit to let her see my bald head.

The Entitled Mother then straight up started yelling in my face. "Stop making excuses and get of the f&#@ing seat you f@$&ing skinhead piece of s**t!"

At this point, I was baffled and didn't know what to say. The kid was trying to make his mother stop and we had the attention of the whole bus. She grabbed me and tried to yank me from my seat. I held on tight and thankfully didn't fall off.

Enter the old gentleman, my savior. "Will you shut the f&#k up you dumb cow?"

"Who do you think you're talking to?" she shrieks.

"Stop assaulting other passengers or I will be forced to step in," he replies in an ice cold voice. "Also, every dumb moron could see that the guy has cancer."

"No, he's just a f&@#ing skinhead."

"He's got no eyebrows you twat!"

Seemed like that *really* offended the Entitled Mother, because she spun around on the spot and threw a falcon punch in old gentleman's face. I was shocked and in disbelief. No, the whole bus was flabbergasted and the kid probably wished he'd never been born. The old gentleman then said something unbelievable and a golden, sweet karma moment followed.

"Ok, that does it. Harassing passengers on the bus, physical assault against a passenger and now assaulting an officer. You're in deep trouble lady."

The old gentleman then pulled out a badge and told her to stay where she was. He called someone on the phone and told her she was being arrested.

I couldn't believe it—the old gentleman was a bloody cop.

The Entitled Mother was as white as a wall. The bus had just come to a stop, so she decided she'd make a run for it but other passengers blocked her way (she then also got charged with resisting arrest thanks to this). Three stops later a police car was waiting for the her and her kid.

The kid told me he was sorry for his mother's behavior and I felt really sorry for the kid (he wasn't a bad child, but his mother was a hell spawn).

The officer then asked me if I wanted to press charges (to which I gladly said yes), took a statement and thankfully was kind enough to let me solve everything on the phone so I didn't have to come to the police station for questioning.

In the end the Entitled Mother got some jail time (I think it was a few months) and some community service. I, in return, got a good story to tell and the sweet taste of instant karma.

Right now, I'm riding the same bus home as I just got back from the hospital after a checkup, which reminded me of this.

The surgery went well—I was declared cancer-free in November and my hair is slowly returning. Also, I don't need to wear a wig anymore.

23

Posted by **the kiwi247**

My son broke his computer, he's allowed to use yours!

I was twelve, my parents moved us to a new place and our neighbors were unpleasant.

There was the Entitled Mother and father (never met him, can't call him entitled), their two sons—one was thirteen and the other was about eight or nine. The older brother was a decent guy. We were school bus pals, but the younger one was an issue. Looking back on it he probably had a social disorder like Asperger's or perhaps ADHD. My mum did not like this kid. A few incidents had happened before, and my mum nicknamed him the *orange-haired goblin.*

This story is told from my mother's perspective, as she dealt with the Entitled Mother. Despite this happening over ten years ago, I do remember that it happened but the written dialogue here is pulled from my mother's retelling of the story, so there's a tad of embellishment.

This was in the day of dial-up in my country. It was fantastic. My mum and I had a system where I'd quickly load a flash game with a heads up, then disconnect from the internet and plug the phone back in. It was the school holidays so it was just my mum and I at home when dad was at work, so it was an otherwise empty house when this happened.

"You're supposed to give a heads up when you're unplugging the phone," my mother said. "I need to make a call."

"I'm not on the computer though," I shouted from the backyard. "I'm outside."

Mum pokes her head out the kitchen window, sees me, looks confused and then turns around. She and I have the same idea, so we both head to the room with the computer and we find the orange-haired goblin.

"Excuse me, what are you doing?" my mum asks him.

"My mum told me I could use your computer," he replies.

Despite hating this kid, my mother is not unreasonable. She's not going to get annoyed with an eight year old. "Why don't you use yours?"

"I broke it."

"Well I'm sorry but she can't decide that," my mum replied. "You have

65

to ask for permission. Besides, you can't let yourself in our house anyway. You can finish the game but I need to plug the phone back in so you can't load anything else."

Mum then gives me a look that meant *keep an eye on him*. She later told me she didn't want him to break our computer if he indeed broke his own, so she needed me to keep an eye on him. The kid eventually leaves, then ten minutes later we hear a knock on the door. I go to answer but my mum gets there first.

"Orange-haired goblin told me you won't let him on your computer," the Entitled Mother said immediately.

"Sorry, who?" my mum asked.

"My son."

"Oh right, the kid who let himself in. He told me you told him he could use my computer. Why is that?"

"His was broken and I needed to entertain him," the Entitled Mother replied.

"So that makes it okay? I wouldn't have minded letting him if you had just discussed it with me first."

"He's an angel, there's no harm in him using it," the Entitled Mother insists.

"Clearly there is if he broke his one."

At this point, the woman must have been getting annoyed. I heard this part for myself as she started shouting very loudly. "He only broke his keyboard, he spilled his drink on it! It's safe for him to use yours because he learned his lesson."

"Still doesn't give him or you the right to come and go as you please and use our property without permission!"

"But you said you would have let him so what's the problem?"

"My problem is a strange kid I barely know just walked into my house and used my computer because 'his mother said he could'. If that's how you treat your neighbors then you or your children aren't welcome here anymore."

My mum then slammed the door, and that was the last we heard from the Entitled Mother, though she'd stare at us if she saw us leave the house. My mum would make jokes about the kid if she saw him in the street, like "crap it's the orange-haired goblin, remember to lock the door".

When school resumed, I was talking to the older brother on the school bus. He told me that his mother asked him to steal our keyboard if he ever comes around again. He understood his mother was a *whackadoodle* so we just had a laugh about it.

A lot of people are wondering how the kid got inside without us knowing. Doors are usually kept unlocked where we live, but we learned our lesson and started locking it after.

24

Posted by **nikknox**

My Daughter invited her 8yo friend to swim in our new pool, and friend brings her toddler sister along with swimsuit on. I told friend sister could swim too, if mom comes to watch her and send her home with that message. EM sends both back again. Repeatedly.

So let me tell y'all about how this Entitled Mother tried to have me be her free babysitter/lifeguard.

We just got one of those above ground pools you setup yourself that is four feet deep and fourteen feet round. We spent the majority of two days prepping and filling it and letting it warm. Finally yesterday it was ready, and my daughter asked if she could invite a little girl she is semi-friendly with from down the street to come swim with her. Since both are eight they are tall enough to stand with heads above water and I said ok.

Well her little friend brought her toddler sister, who is probably on the younger side of two. Definitely too small to stand with head above the water.

I tell friend that little sister can't get in the water unless her mom is here to watch her, and send her home with the message. They both come back. "Mom said she's fine in her float and I can watch her."

And I said, "No it's not fine, I do not think an eight year old is responsible enough to watch a toddler in a pool and I am not going to be the one watching her either. You need to tell your mom either she comes to watch your little sister or she is not getting in the pool."

They both go home and then *both come back!*

At this point I am livid and walk back to their house with them and pound on the door. No answer.

I keep knocking, and then the garage door starts to open with this woman backing her car out! I quickly went and stood at the end of the driveway with all the kids in tow, both of hers and both of mine.

She gets out of her car all pissed off and asks me what my problem is!

I tell her my problem is that I'm not her babysitter, and that I am definitely not going to be responsible for keeping her baby from drowning in *my* swimming pool on *my* property!

She then proceeds to start baby talking her own kids saying, "I'm so sorry babies, the mean lady isn't going to let you swim. I'm so sorry princesses" and on and on.

Of course toddler bursts into tears, and then the Entitled Mother screams at me. "Look what you've done! You've made her cry and ruined her day! Hope you are proud of yourself!"

She then snatches up little sister who is screaming and tosses her in the car, and screams at friend to get in too.

Friend is red in the face, and you can tell she is so embarrassed and just mumbles "sorry" while climbing in the car. The Entitled Mother then proceeds to peel out of her own driveway and we walk back home.

Bitch.

CHOOSING BEGGARS

Ah, the paradox that is the choosing beggar.

The r/ChoosingBeggars subreddit loosely defines one as a *"Person seeking goods or services at a reduced cost, for free, or for a laughably lopsided trade or Person using social media, dating apps, or otherwise to seek out a specific type of relationship and must have unreasonable standards or have a comical sense of entitlement"*. Not someone with a run of bad luck.

The distinction is pretty simple:
If you're having a bad month and ask friends and family for grocery money that's begging, and it happens to the best of us.
If you get offended by the amount you are offered, demand more to buy a specific brand of organic lemons and scoff at the notion of paying it back then you're a Choosing beggar.

Sheer bloody audacity is the thought that comes to mind when dealing with these people, because no matter how egregious their behavior they all without fail somehow either think they are owed something or they are in the right.

25

CB mom demands access to my swimming pool

I had this rather amazing run-in with a choosing beggar last week, and boy was it entertaining and infuriating.

I'm renting a single story house with a private swimming pool with my wife. The house is part of a small "neighborhood" of six houses in total, two of which are slightly bigger than the others and have a private pool each. Those two are a fair bit more expensive for obvious reasons.

Last week someone knocks on the door and I go to open it. Outside is a smiling woman with two kids.

"Hello, I'm Sandra from next door," she said. "We thought we'd use the pool."

"Oh you did, did you?" I replied, confused as hell and a bit stunned. I now also notice that they're all carrying towels and have swim suits on. "I don't really like lending it out, I'm afraid, so I think I'll have to say no."

"Oh, but the rent gives me access to the pool when I want," she replied smugly, as if she's calling me an idiot.

"You're not paying the rent for my house, and I know the owner doesn't include use of the pool in the contract." I know this because he's a close friend of my wife and I happen to be the one who wrote the contract, as well as having translated the guy's ads for Facebook and such.

"Well it's in the lease, so you don't really have any choice, do you?"

At this point I just ask my wife to call up the owner, and he confirms that he hasn't said anything about her being allowed to use the pool and that the contract doesn't mention it.

I tell her this, but since she has kids I tell her that I'll allow her to come over to use the pool perhaps once a month, as long as she gives me one week's notice or so. This is not good enough for Sandra, who demands immediate access to the pool as well as future use whenever she feels like it.

This of course results in me withdrawing my kind offer, and her stomping away screaming about getting me kicked out. Later, the owner shows up (having heard her screaming through the phone) and warns her sternly that *she* will be kicked out if she makes any more trouble.

I don't think she'll be staying here for long.

26

Posted by **Ripped Trousers**

Lady wants a free pizza, then refuses it

I used to work at a little pizzeria and after a busy night we'd sometimes end up with a couple of mistake pizzas that we couldn't sell sitting on top of the oven. Like if the cook accidentally put on the wrong toppings or a slightly burned pizza, stuff like that.

One night about twenty minutes before closing a lady comes in and proceeds to tell me a sob story about her and her son being stranded and hungry, having nothing to eat all day and asking can I give her a free pizza.

"You're in luck," I say cheerfully. "I actually do have an extra pizza tonight and you can have it."

"Can I see it?" she asks, so I took the pizza box off the oven and showed her a perfectly fine pepperoni and mushroom pizza. "Ew, it's got mushrooms on it."

Surprised at how picky she was I replied, "I guess so . . ."

"Can you make me a different pizza?"

"Not for free. If you want a pizza to order I have to charge you for it."

"But I don't have any money!" she wails.

"So take this free one then!"

"But I don't like mushrooms!"

"You can pick them off," I reply.

A look of disgust rolls over her face. "I don't want that one. Can't you give me anything else?"

"Sorry, this is the only thing I can give you for free."

She sighs angrily and just walks out, doesn't take the pizza. I guess they weren't that hungry!

27

Posted by **EnjoyYourMealYouToo**

Psycho Family Demands & Damages my £4000 PC

I'm a pretty hardcore PC Gamer.

When I turned seventeen I got a job. Saved my first pay packet for a few months and spent two thousand pounds on a PC. Over the past five years I kept upgrading it, spending about four thousand on it in total over that time. Six months ago I was having massive issues and it turned out my graphics card has fried.

I had been saving for a new PC and spent a lot more on that, so I had a spare cooked PC in my room. I swapped out parts and turned it into a mini server to run in my room. All good.

This Christmas we had family at our place including the young children. My cousin who's eleven was looking in my room as it's quite techy so naturally he's interested. This child and his brother are not technically minded. They don't have mobiles, IPads, game consoles or even internet. They're very strange children and they're kind of the weird family you're forced to invite to gatherings because they're family.

He notices my mini-server and says, "Wow you have two computers."

I basically just agree to save the effort of explaining the difference to him. He then tells me he wishes he has one and just stares at me like I'm the reason he hasn't got his own.

I chuckle it off and we go back downstairs to the party. Later on my aunt (his mum) comes up to me and asks why I need two computers. I explain to her about one being my main PC and another being a server. She does the "technophobe hands", which are the jazz hands people do when you explain something technological to them. She asks if the choosing beggar cousin could have the PC so he can play Fortnite and Pokemon.

Not that I need a reason, but:

1.) It's mine, no.
2.) It's a server, not a standard PC.
3.) They also have no internet or knowledge of how to set up a PC.

I basically just flatly say no, sorry and she storms off almost in a tantrum. Now I consider us a normal-type family and these things just don't happen. I told my dad (who doesn't like them) and he just laughs loudly. We're getting weird now.

My choosing beggar cousin literally sits in my room, leaning against my server under the desk for probably five hours. I ask him to come back down and he just says no he's comfortable and just sits there.

So it gets to about ten in the evening and people are leaving. The choosing beggar aunt & uncle get their things and get ready to go, then say the kid won't leave without the "PC". They look at me like this is my fault and I'm wondering where the discipline is. The Aunt finally goes upstairs to get him while the rest of us kind of sit awkwardly silent in the hallway.

They're gone about five minutes.

I mean it's not a big house, grab that little shit's hands and pull him downstairs. Eventually I go up to see what the issue is and the kid is *literally* mounting my server. He has his arms and legs *wrapped* around it, all the cables pulled out and on the floor everywhere and it's halfway across the room where he obviously tried to drag it. Cables are clipped, cables that have been yanked out, so all broken. Let me remind you this child is almost twelve.

I was almost immediately being pinged by my discord from players letting me know my game servers had gone down. For those who don't know about servers, pulling the plug is *very* bad as they need to be shut down properly. I just shout loudly to "get the F out".

The madness peaks at this point as my cousin looks up at me and hisses. Yes, *hisses*. Like a cat or a fat snake.

The choosing beggar aunt starts accusing me of "greed to the highest degree" and drags the cousin from the room to where basically fifteen people are waiting to see the result of the carnage. They then tell me I'll be receiving a bill for the therapy the kid will likely need after a traumatic event I caused which could have been "easily avoided".

As for the server, I needed to buy new cables and one of the storage drives had shattered when he let it fall over. After about a week everything was back to normal.

For those asking why I didn't send them a bill for the damage caused, it was about a hundred and fifty pounds to repair. Neither of them work so they wouldn't be able to afford it and the stress of small claims isn't worth it as I have some money set aside each month for anything tech or reptile related I own which breaks.

Since then I've joined my dad & brother in non-contact with the psycho family. *But,* there's a little bit extra.

Last week I received a random Facebook message from a page called "PC Donations" asking me if I had any spare PC's to donate to children who weren't as fortunate in my local area (a small town). A page that had been created about two hours prior and had zero likes and activity.

Genius.

28

Guy wanted me to make him a queen-size blanket.

(Text conversation)

Wed 11:18PM
Hey! Your blankets are amazing do you do commissions?

Today 12:12PM
Hello?

> Hi! Sorry. I've been out of town with my fiancé. Haven't been on Instagram much.

Well that's not a very good business practice.

> I beg your pardon?

Not responding to potential clients.

> I'm sorry. As I said. I was out of town with my fiancé.
> Is there something I can do for you.

Yes. A commission that's why I messaged you in the first place.

> Ok...

I want a blanket. In a cathrines wheel stitch. You know what that is right?
Light Grey, light blue and cream.
Oh and I would like it made out of natural fiber like wool or alpaca. None of that acrylic shit.

> What size? And I'm going to need to know what type of fiber you want because there's a big cost difference in wool, alpaca, and "acrylic shit".

Wool.
And it's going to be a blanket for the couch so it needs to be big enough for

two people to be under.
So let's say 6'x7'

> So you want basically a queen sized blanket
> Give me a couple hours and I'll get back to you on a price

Okay..

> Are you wanting thick or regular yarn

Regular? I don't want it super bulky.

> Okay, I can make the blanket for $400. I require %50 up
> front and the other %50 upon completion. It will probably
> take me 3-4 weeks to complete.

…
Are you for real??

> Yeah

That is an insane amount of money for a fucking blanket. I can literally go
to Walmart and get a blanket for $15.

> Then go to Walmart and get a blanket

…
Seriously
How the fuck did you get that price???
For a blanket???

> You want a blanket that is 100% wool. Not acrylic or
> anything artificial. I'll blanket the size you want who's
> going to require roughly 4200 yards of yarn. Which would
> require me to buy 20 skeins of wool. The wool is $8 per
> skien.

That would come out to $160 then not $400.
Plus craft stores are always having sales so you could probably get the yarn
for A LOT less.

> The other $240 is for my time

That's insane.
You're charging way too much.

> You want a wool blanket that is essentially queen size made of wool. You want a complex stitch that works up extremely slowly. A blanket as large as you are requesting in such a slow stitch will take me 120-150 hours. You're telling me that charging less than $2 an hour is "Charging way too much"?

Other crocheters can make it for so much cheaper.

> Then have it made by other crocheters.

You are insane.
I can't believe you think $400 is a fair price
I need this blanket made.
It's for my girlfriend.
She's super ill and I want her to have something nice.

> That's unfortunate but it's still going to cost you $400

You're insane
You should give me a friends and family discount or something since you took forever to respond to me.

> I charge friends and family more

I'll tell you what. Here's what we are going to do. You make the blanket. Get the yard on sale. ON SALE ONLY. When it's completed I will pay you. But only when it's completed I'll give you $70. Which is more than generous.

> No. You pay me $200 up front and $200 upon completion. Then you pay shipping.

Why the fuck do I pay half up front.
???

> Because if you back out I'm not $160 in the hole on yarn.

Your insane.
I gave you a really generous offer.
I'm going to report you.
I'll make sure everyone knows of your scam.
You are charging way to much.
WAY TO MUCH.

> Oh no. Nobody will ever ask me to do a commission
> again! Don't do that! I'm begging you

Your going to be going out of business.

> Oh. My. Gosh.

You don't believe me?

> Oh no. I do
> I just don't care

Fuck you. I will destroy your business.

> Dude. I don't have a business. I'm a fucking flight
> instructor. Crochet is just my hobby. I take commissions
> on occasion but I don't do crochet for an income. I don't
> even really want commissions that much. So if you want
> the damn blanket then that's what I'm charging.

Fuck you.
Then you should do it for free.
You don't need the money.

> Tell you what. I'll do it for $800.

29

Posted by **ShieraBlackwood**

"Fire her so that I can have my old job back!"

A few years ago, I had the pleasure of working with "Kim".

Kim had an administrative job at our shared place of business, and we worked together for about a year. She wasn't a great employee, mainly due to attitude and a constant stream of missed time for assorted reasons, most of which seemed to be bullshit.

Kim eventually found her "dream job", which we discovered after she failed to call or show up for three days straight. We parted amicably enough, even allowing her to "resign" to avoid ending things on a negative note, and that was the end of that.

In Kim's absence, "Lee" had been promoted and quickly proved to be excellent at the job. Consequently, we weren't really all that excited when Kim reappeared about a week after her departure, sobbing and begging for her job back. The "dream job" hadn't been very dreamy after all, and she was running low on funds.

Moved by her pleas on behalf of her children, the manager agreed to bring her back on a trial basis to fill the vacancy left when Lee was promoted. It was step down from her previous position, but it was immediately available.

A short, very blunt conversation ensued where she demanded to know why she couldn't just have her old job back. We explained, again, that the position had been filled and that the entry level spot we were offering was the only thing available. We pointed out that she'd been a no-call, no-show and that she'd burned a lot of bridges with the company by the poor way she'd handled her departure. The offer of *any* position with the company again was a kindness, pure and simple.

"Well, the only reason I came back was because I figured you'd miss me and want me back," was her reply. "I don't really think I need to take a step down, do you?"

This resulted in a long silence. I was on the verge of telling her to just forget about it when she got up to leave. She seemed to sense she was pushing her luck. "I really appreciate the opportunity! Maybe some doors will open for me, and I will be able to move back up soon!"

Whatever. I half expected her to blow it off and just never come back.

She came in late the following day, and accomplished almost nothing. Instead, she divided her time between hovering over Lee and hiding in the break room with her cell phone. After being asked repeatedly to return to her work, she abruptly left without a word.

The next day, she didn't come in at all. We left a voicemail at the end of the day informing her that her employment had been terminated and that her final check would be mailed.

The following day, she arrived bright and early and demanded a meeting with the manager. Upon being told that she would not get a meeting, and that she was not welcome on the premises, she threw a massive tantrum in full view of the office. She said that it was "unfair" that we'd "taken her job away" and given it to Lee, that she had kids to feed and that we needed to be "nicer".

We explained that she wasn't entitled to the job, and that she had squandered all of her bargaining power by walking out *twice*. Furthermore, the job was taken—it was now Lee's.

She then dropped her purse, shouting the immortal line "So just fire her so that I can have it back!"

It was one of those moments that just sticks with you.

We were all kind of shocked at her audacity and single-minded selfishness. Lee was really uncomfortable (as you can imagine), and quickly left the room. Without saying much of anything, I picked up Kim's purse, handed it to her and walked her out. She sat outside for a long time, then left.

She called back six months later and asked if we were ready to "give her a fair chance".

We declined.

30

My step sister in law wanted me to leave everything I have to her kids.

My step sister in law is the kind of person who couldn't fathom why any woman would not want to become a mother. She's always been really critical of my choice to be childfree. She made some catty comments about how I'll never know true happiness.

However when I saw her a few days ago at my dad's birthday party she seemed to have done a complete one eighty.

She told me again and again how she's supportive of my life choices and shouldn't have kids if I don't want them. I didn't know what to make of this. I just said something like "oh okay, thanks" but my gut told me that there was more to her sudden acceptance than she was letting on.

The phone call I received from her yesterday proved my gut instincts right.

She started off with the usual "how are you . . . we need to get together soon . . ." bullshit. Then, she began to not so subtly inquire about my finances (what sort of savings do I have, how much I make every year etc.). I of course got irritated and asked her what she meant and to come to the point.

She giggled. "Well . . . since you won't be having kids of your own, why don't you make my children your heirs?"

I didn't know whether to laugh like a maniacal villain or just get pissed. I decided to let her go on.

"As you know your brother and I are planning to have at least four kids (they already have 1)," she continued. "So when they're born you can leave equal portions of your estate to all of them.

"Uh huh."

"You and that boyfriend of yours say you don't even want to get married. So it's not like you *have* to leave anything to him, right?"

"Really?"

"Yeah. So I thought instead of your life savings going to waste they can just go to your family."

"After I'm dead," I replied flatly.

"Yes."

"Do you plan to make it look like suicide, or an accident?"

"Uh, what?" she mutters, clearly confused.

"Since you've planned all of this you must have made some plans to off me right? Go on, tell me what it is. Is it something super creative and unusual?"

Angry in the way that douchebags get when you call them out on their bullshit, she scoffs. "How could you think that? I only suggested this so you wouldn't have the burden of worrying about what would happen to your money when you're on your deathbed."

"Aren't you a sweetheart! I'll spare *you* the burden of worrying about me worrying about my money by leaving everything I have to charities that I support."

She started blabbering again, but before she could form a full sentence I hung up. I also called my dad to let him know about this.

This morning, I received a call from my step brother and he apologized profusely for what his wife had said. I told him if she ever pulled anything like this again it will be the last time I speak to them.

31

Posted by **Silver Tongue64**

No, I'm not making you another one.

I work at a supermarket, stocking the shelves at night. It pays well and I enjoy the work, but some people think it's a mediocre job. Which it sort of is.

Anyway, this particular store is run by a guy who is so cheap that at Christmas and Yule he won't even give the night crew anything as a reward. It's obnoxious of me to assume we deserve something like that, but literally every other store's crew received a pizza feast with soda and ice cream as a reward for being so good to the store the whole year.

Our manager at our store didn't do this for us, like every other year, so that his end of year bonus is bigger.

To make up for it, I cook and bake for my crew. Sometimes I make sweet things, sometimes something savory. This year I made mini-lasagnas for everyone and a few people on the day crew I liked. And I say mini, but I mean each is around twelve by four inches. So not that small.

I skip out on sleep and buy the good ingredients so that everyone has something tasty. Everyone loves them, except this one girl, who I'll call Rabbit. She got her lasagna and a small bag of cookies as a bonus and had the nerve to ask me why it was so small.

This damn lasagna is around four pounds of deliciousness and she's a very small person. She tells me that it wouldn't be near enough for both her and her husband and that I should bring her a much bigger one. She fully intended on keeping the first.

I explained that I made around fourteen lasagnas and that my oven and my time were not enough for more than that. This still wasn't good enough.

She tells me that she and her husband are going to go hungry for Christmas day dinner and that I should feel bad. I told her that she deserved nothing and that next time she won't be getting anything.

Later in the day she had the nerve to tell me that the lasagna was delicious and she looks forward to the next one.

This is what you get for being nice. And also, who the hell eats a lasagna that big in less than four hours!

32

Posted by **omegaweapon**

2 weeks....

(Text conversation)

Hi there, I was wondering what the turn around time for a custom desk is. I need the height to be 700mm. Width enough to fit triple 24" monitors side by side. I'd like a keyboard sized area at the front slanted forward for ease of typing/gaming

> Hiya, I have a template for that exact design. Around 2 weeks before we can start it currently.

Oh, can you do it sooner by any chance? I was referred by *(Removed)*.

> I'm sorry 2 weeks from now is the best I can do at the moment. We're quite busy as *(Removed)* stopped importing and rely on us now

Thankyou. I'll inform *(Removed)* that you weren't helpful at all and they'll pull the contract.
How long now?

> Still 2 weeks

I will seriously notify Mark and I will advise him to not use you anymore if you can't do better than 2 weeks.
??

> ......dos weeks

I'm not joking
??

> Hold a second, I'm on the phone with Mark

You are not

He said 2 weeks
??
He's calling you now
Hello?

I can't believe you actually snitched to him. You don't even know my name?

I said "some due with (your number) is saying he wants to discuss pulling our mutually beneficial contract Mark. Would you like to chat with him?"
Okay look, I'll do you a favour since you're so nice

So how long already?

I just re-checked my schedule

And???
Well????

Hang on just crunching some numbers

If you say 2 weeks I swear
????

I better not say anything then, I wouldn't want you to swear

Just say it!! What the hell is wrong with you?
Oh my god??? How long does it take?
Never mind. Screw you

.....3 weeks

Fuck you

33

Posted by **Topcorjor**

*Ex Fiancée cheated on me, and then asked what she was entitled to...
from my mom's house.*

Buckle in, kiddos. This is gonna be a weird one.

So in my late teens I met a girl who I swore was the one. At the time, she was the first girl I ever dated that I had an actual real relationship with. I was young and very naive. She was the first girl I ever said "I love you" to, and I thought that meant it was a forever deal.

Things were awesome for a couple years. Then, she started a second job at a liquor store to make some extra money so that she could afford to buy a car and start thinking about moving out of her mom's place. Admirable, I thought.

I totally supported her on that one. I was still living at home with my mom, and the construction job I worked at definitely didn't pay enough to move out and afford a car. With her working two jobs, though, we could definitely afford a place of our own.

After a few months of working this liquor store job (and one robbery that a guy punched her in the head), she started acting different. I chalked it up to the robbery incident. That messed her up a bit.

It didn't ring any massive alarms, but she had bought a car and started giving one of her male coworker's rides home after her shift was over. I thought nothing of it. It was what it was.

I found out from not only her coworkers but her best friend that she had been cheating on me with this guy once they left work. When I confronted her about it, she cried and denied it. I was in love. I believed her. I just thought it was jealous rumors.

A friend of mine brought up going to Mexico for a trip with the guys. I had never been on a plane before, let alone been out of Canada, so I was all over that. I had a bit of money saved up from work, so four of us went . . . without my girlfriend.

While in Mexico, I cheated.

I feel so bad about it to this day, but back then (fifteen years ago) I guess I was just trying to get back at her.

When I got back to Canada, I felt so guilty that I went right to a jewelry store and bought an engagement ring. So stupid. Yes, I Chandler Bing'd it. She said yes, and life was all good again.

We were engaged for a year and a half. She was still living with her mom, I was still living with mine.

During this time, she broke up with me four times over the dumbest stuff.

She came over to my place once, and her clothes weren't dry from when I had put them in the wash. Close, but not quite. She opened up the dryer, grabbed her clothes and stormed out. She dumped me when she got home. That was the first time. I was crushed.

It happened a couple times after that, but they weren't that serious. I wasn't worried.

Things went okay after those three times. The final time we broke up, I was out of town on a business training course. I called her from my hotel on Valentine's Day, asking how she wanted to celebrate.

"We need to talk".

That's how she started every breakup.

By this point, I was done. She said she didn't know if this is what she wanted with her life, yadda yadda. I agreed. I didn't want a girl who was going to break up with me every time she was upset. I told her to come over when I got back, bring me the ring and I'll give her whatever she left at my mom's place.

Simple, yes?

Not so much. This is where she goes stupid.

She shows up to my mom's house with her mom in tow. She gives me the ring, I hand her some clothes she left, some shampoo and a copy of *The Notebook* on DVD that I paid for but didn't want. She looked confused.

I asked her what the problem was. She dead ass looked me right in the face. "Shouldn't I get more?"

I thought I misheard her. I asked her what she meant.

"Well we were engaged so I should get more stuff," she replied. "I'm entitled to half, right?"

I burst out laughing.

Not even kidding, as heartbroken as I knew I was going to be over the next little while, that was the moment that I had zero love or respect for her.

We talked for a bit with her mom (nobody else was home at my house) who also thought that she was entitled to more than her belongings. After about five minutes of them pointing at things in my mom's house and saying they want it, I kicked them out. My last words to her as she stood by the front step looking like she wanted to fix things was, "Bye, good luck. You're gonna need it. Both of you."

Bullet successfully dodged. Wow. To this day that still floors me. How the fuck do you think you deserve my mom's belongings, especially when we don't even live together?

34

Posted by **lovestosnooj**

Give me your laptop (Not my laptop) since you have 2 (one is my wife's)

I work in IT, Web Dev stuff, so I know my way around a PC and my neighbors know this.

A week ago or so one of them comes to my door and says that they bought a laptop but it wasn't starting up. I told her that I don't really know laptop hardware and only open up PCs so I can look if something is wrong with the software then I can probably fix it, but if it's hardware then she would need to go to a shop.

I invite CB to enter because I want to get it over with instantly and not have to go drop the laptop off at her house.

I turn it on, nothing. Not even a light. Nothing works. The charging light is on but the laptop is dead.

I told her she would have to go to a shop because this is not a software issue. She mumbles but leaves without saying thanks, which I didn't really care about—I just wanted my peace and quiet.

Yesterday she rings the door I open and there she is, with the laptop in hand. I will paraphrase the conversation.

"I just got back from the store," she began, unprompted, "they said the motherboard is dead."

"Sorry to hear that. It's a shame, can't you get a ref—"

"No! I wanted to ask about your laptops . . ."

"Ok," I begin carefully. "What about mine?"

"Well, can you give me one of them? She asks. "I need it for my kids and they don't have anything to play on."

"No I can't give you a laptop because that is my work laptop, bought and paid from the company I work at . . . it's not mine."

"Oh, c'mon. Just tell them you lost it or someone stole it." She then proceeds to laugh.

"I would get fired if that happened." I really would, there is sensitive information on that laptop.

Undeterred, she asks, "Well, what about the other one?"

"That's my wife's laptop."

"Give me that one. It's perfect for me."

At this point I was fuming, but this person is a close neighbor and friend to my mom. "I can't give you my wife's laptop. She bought it, it's hers. Go return the laptop to where you bought it."

"*They will not refund me,*" she insists. "They say it's my fault for not checking it before buying it."

Mind you, she bought it second hand.

"Well, yes, it's your fault. I have to go, but good luck with that."

I slammed the door when she started to talk again. I really didn't have time to deal with her crazy today.

These people, how entitled are they to think I can just give away or lie to my job?

35

I teach swimming to kids for free even though i was offered money. Mombie demands that I have to teach her son exclusively. And to give her the money offered as i don't need it.

(Text conversation)

Hello. You are the lady who teaches swimming right? I got your number from Sangeetha. Can you teach my son also? **10:08**

Yes. Sure. **10:10**

She said she offered to pay but it is free. Is that true? I can't pay. **10:11**
Free right?? **10:20**
I can't pay. I am single mom **10:41**
Hello? **10:57**
Please reply **11:05**
?? **11:20**
Hello? Ter? **11:30**

Hey. Yes, they are free. I am in office. I won't be able to respond right away. **11:35**

Wow. That's rude. **11:35**
I want to know what time today I should bring my son to the pool **11:36**

I am sorry but today I already informed everyone that I wanted to swim alone today. I will message you the next time I am teaching. Probably, after 3 days. **11:59**
I usually teach the kids from 3-5pm. **12:00**

Can you come at 1 today and teach him? 1 – 3 is more warm than 3 – 5. I know you have flexible timing. **12:01**
Can you reply faster? **12:06**

I can't teach at 1 because of work. It is already past 12. And today, I really feel stressed and I need to blow off some steam. I don't want to teach today. I already told everyone that. From next time, I will inform you also. **12:07**

That's not fair. I already told him that he can go swimming today. **12:07**
Give me one good reason to tell him. Else, he is gonna cry. **12:08**

1. I am not teaching today.
2. I already cancelled. I can't un-cancel with everyone this late. **12:11**

That's even better. You can teach him alone. Those brats got free classes for a month. You need to make up for that with my son. **12:12**

What? **12:13**
I can't teach just for your son. **12:13**

Why not? He has anxiety issues. You have to teach him alone. **12:13**

I am not a certified trainer. I don't want to be responsible for the safety of a kid with anxiety in a pool with depth twice his size. I think you should get someone else. **12:15**

When I say anxiety, ILi don't mean like that. He just doesn't like other kids. **12:16**
Just teach him exclusively for one month. After that, you can put him with everyone . they got more classes than him. It is not fair. **12:17**
So you start teaching him from tomorrow. At 1. It is better to be out of the pool by 3. That way no one gets sick. **12:19**
Also, he doesn't have goggle. Bring a extra pair tomorrow or let him use yours until I buy one. **12:20**

I can't swim daily. If I go swimming today, it will be at least 2 days before I swim again. And, I am not gonna teach anyone exclusively. **12:21**

Wow. You are such a selfish bitch. He is just a kid. Don't you have any heart. I am a single mom. And I already told him. **12:21**
So... **12:24**
Tomorrow at 1? **12:25**
I can see that you have seen my messages. **12:28**
I will throw him in the pool tomorrow at 1. If something happens to him

you are responsible.   **12:29**

Whatever. You are probably a lousy teacher.   **12:32**

You are such a nasty horrible person. My son doesn't this. I don't know what I did to deserve this. Why is everyone so selfish and unhelpful these days.   **12:47**

You have flexible timings. You work less hours than me. You earn more than me. Those bitches are rich enough that they can afford to get a swimming instructor but no. they want only free stuff that my son needs. **12:49**

You are so priveledged that you don't need money. You fucking refuse money that people are ready to pay. They are ready to give money and you don't need money. Do you know how much I need that money? I am a single mom. You should get the money from them and give it to me.

You are priveledged. You should give it to me. I need it more than you. If you won't teach my son alone you should ateast give the money to me. **12:53**

Reply me. I can see that you read the message. Bitch   **12:55**

PRO REVENGE

Revenge is a dish best served cold. That's the old adage.

If you think about it, couching revenge in cooking terms just works. Both require planning and preparation, knowing how long to simmer for and getting the steps just right. Some call for cool, refreshing notes while others need to be fiery and full of attitude.

r/ProRevenge is all about people getting righteous justice against those who have wronged them, usually in an elaborate, imaginative and hilariously poetic manner.

No two cooks are the same and no two people have the same taste. Personally, when it comes to revenge I do away with the cold preperation and opt for mine served often and without mercy.

36

Posted by **RockyMoose**

Landlord is jealous of my income, raises my rent $500. I screw him years later for $20k.

In the late nineties the wife and I were just married and getting started, so we decided to DINK ("double income, no kids") it for a few years to save up for a down payment on a house.

The dotcom bubble was still rising and I was a newly minted software developer. I had an entry-level job for a while and then got recruited to a new city and a new job that paid three times what I was making before. It was an offer too good to pass up. I ran the numbers and it was a no-brainer; by living frugally and saving my entire salary, living off just her income, we would easily have enough in a year to put down a twenty percent payment upfront on a new house.

We rented an apartment in the new city that was listed for nine hundred and fifty dollars a month. The landlord was a real estate agent who owned a two-bedroom condo as an investment property. Let's call him Hank Wazowski. Hank was a thin, gray, no-nonsense guy. He was pleasant enough, but perfunctory, dry, and had no sense of humor. He made a point of explaining that under no circumstances was he responsible for maintaining the garbage disposal, that it was *not* included in the rental agreement and he would not be responsible for fixing it if it broke. Um, ok.

Hank seemed slightly amused by us—a clueless, young, newlywed couple, but I could tell he wanted to rent to us because we were very obviously a safe choice as renters.

We filled out the rental agreement and the credit check, and this is where my troubles began.

Hank looked hard at the credit application where I listed my job title, "Software Developer", and my income, seventy five thousand dollars a year. For a twenty three year old in his second year out of college, in the late nineties, this is a small fortune. Throw in my wife's salary and we were over six figures in income, renting an apartment far beneath our means. Like I said, DINK is the way to go when starting out.

"I can't believe how much money you make," Hank must have said half a dozen times between muttering under his breath.

I explained we were saving to buy a house and that we were only going to stay in the apartment a year. "We might stay a few months after the term is over, would month-to-month be ok after a year?"

Hank assured us that would be fine.

We saw Hank only once during the year and he again mentioned my salary and how he couldn't believe that's what software developers were making. It was awkward and I gave a vague reply.

Anyway, a year later we had found a house to buy, signed all the papers and were making plans to move. The new house wasn't going to be ready until two months after our rental lease was up, so I called Hank to ask if we could, as discussed, simply extend the lease by two months before moving out. Hank assured me on the phone it would be no problem and he would send over an extension for us to sign. The extension arrived in the mail and it included a month-to-month clause and a $500 increase in the rent.

I flipped out and called him. "Hank, why are you increasing the rent by over fifty percent. That's too much! That's more than my new mortgage is going to be!"

His reply was super condescending. "RockyMoose, it's what the apartment goes for now. I would be losing money by renting it for less." I tried to reason with him but it was very clear he knew we could afford the five hundred extra, had no choice in the matter and he was going to screw us over as best he could. He got angry with me for arguing my point, and I'll never forget his parting words. "You don't have to like it, RockyMoose, you just have to pay it."

My wife and I tried to figure a way to move out early by putting our furniture in storage for a couple months and crashing with friends, but it just wasn't going to work out.

I swallowed my pride and wrote out the check for fourteen hundred and fifty for the extra month. A month later I wrote a similar check, and then we moved out. I made sure the apartment was spotless before moving, but still Hank withheld three hundred dollars from our security deposit for bullshit things that were just a way for him to squeeze a few more dollars from the kids who made too much money. A hundred dollars for cleaning? Sure, but three hundred was obscene. In my mind, he had screwed me over for a thousand two hundred dollars and there was nothing I could do about it.

What made is even more infuriating is that I saw the advert Hank put in the paper after we moved out and he listed the apartment for rent at only a hundred and fifty more than we had been paying originally, not the grossly-inflated five hundred dollar increase. And it didn't rent. A month later I saw the same ad and he had lowered the price to seventy five more than we had been paying, and I assume it got rented since the ads stopped appearing.

Fast-forward about five years. Life is good, the house is good, we have a baby and even though the dotcom bubble has burst I'm still employed. One day, out of the blue, I overhear one of my co-workers, Phil, a senior developer, talking to the guy working the reception desk. "Hey, Mike, I'm expecting someone to drop off some paperwork for me. If a Hank Wazowski asks for me, tell him I'll be right out."

I freeze and get a taste of bile in my mouth remembering how I had to write out that name on those checks all those years ago. There's no way it's the same guy, right? I walk over to Phil who is still by the reception desk.

"Phil," I say, "How do you know that name, Hank Wazowski?"

He explains that Hank is his real estate agent. "I bought my condo through him several years ago. I'm selling my condo now so I can buy a house. So I'm going to ask him to be my agent again. Do you know him?"

I tell Phil that I used to rent an apartment from Hank and described what he looks like. Phil confirms the description. It's the same guy, wow small world, right? And on cue, right then the front door to the office opens and in walks Hank Wazowski. I stare in disbelief. He's carrying a folder of papers and doesn't recognize me.

Phil and Hank shake hands and they talk for a few moments. I stand there silently, wondering what to do. Phil finally says, "Hank, this is my friend RockyMoose. I think you may have already met?"

"Yes, hello Hank," I said quickly. "Good to see you again. My wife and I were your tenants a few years ago. Remember, the software developer who rented for a year saving to buy a house? Well, this is where I work. Here. With Phil."

Hanks eyes indicate he now remembers me, and he's starting to put it all together. We shake hands and he says yes, of course he remembers and asks how we are doing.

"Oh we're just fine, thanks for asking. Phil says that you're his real estate agent. Small world, isn't it?" I ask.

Hanks nods pleasantly. He still doesn't remember the details of our last conversation. I do some quick math in my head. This is the early-mid two thousands, the real estate market is very strong and easy money for any agent. The crash of two thousand and eight is still a few years in the future.

I start to think out loud. "Selling the condo for around a hundred and fifty to two hundred thousand, and you're looking at houses in the half a million range, so that's almost seven hundred thousand in total transactions. An agent getting three percent on the sale *and* the purchase is getting around twenty thousand for his trouble. That's a good commission for the agent, isn't it?"

Hanks eyes flash and I can tell he remembers everything about me now. Phil is surprised at my passive-aggressive tone. I am enjoying the uncomfortable silence. Hank deflects my question, saying it's complicated and tells Phil to send back the papers as soon as possible. He shakes hands with Phil, looks at me, nods and turns to leave.

"It was really good to see you again, Hank." I call behind him. As the door is still shutting, I say a bit too loudly, so that Hank can hear, "Phil, don't sign anything just yet, I have a story to tell you."

Phil looks at me and says, "Rocky, what the hell was that all about?!" He looks pissed and confused at my behavior.

I tell Phil the whole story, the rent, the outrageous increase, the security deposit. "You don't have to like it, you just have to pay it." Everything.

"Phil, you can't use this guy to sell your condo and buy a house," I said afterward. "I hate him. He's evil. I'll help you find another real estate agent, just use *anyone but Hank!*"

The great thing about Phil is that, well, he's a great guy. He says he's a little surprised at my story and has always known Hank as a straightforward guy.

"But I totally see him doing that to you," he admits. "There's no way I could use him now. What a dick!" Then Phil's eyes lit up a bit. "What do you want me to say when I fire him?"

I have special feelings for Phil now.

We came up with a plan and I made sure there were some key phrases in Phil's repertoire. We planned it all out together in advance. My only regret is that I didn't get to see Hank's reaction in person a day later when Phil made the following phone call while I stood behind him listening.

"Hi, Hank? It's Phil calling. Yeah, about that. I've decided to get some other quotes from other agents. I'm not going to sign up with you."

[Hank speaks]

"No, no. You shouldn't give a discount. You'd be losing money if you did that."

[Hank speaks]

"This is just a decision I've made . . . no, it has nothing to do with RockyMoose."

[Hank speaks]

"Well, you don't have to like it, Hank. You just have to accept it. Good bye."

CLICK

And it was the greatest revenge I could have ever imagined—through a chance meeting years later, Hank got screwed out of twenty thousand dollars in easy commissions. And the best part is Hank absolutely *knew* it had *everything* to do with RockyMoose!

37

Posted by **fox-mcleod**

Nathan vs. the IRS

First, you have to appreciate the kind of guy Nathan is. Brilliant engineer and slightly crazy person. Nathan likes rules and he doesn't give up when he knows how things should work. I like to get him to tell this story whenever we're together because he doesn't even see why it's funny—it's just how he deals with all problems.

Nathan was like if you saw Sysiphus and you thought, *maybe I should try to stop him.* Then one day the boulder was on top of the hill, and you go and ask Sysiphus how he did it and he replied, "It was simple. I just kept pushing it forever and ever, and eventually . . . the mountain gave up." A real grade nineteen bureaucrat. He just works systematically through problems no matter how daunting they seem.

Until one day, when Nathan's unstoppable force met an immovable object.

I came into work and saw checks and envelopes spread all over his desk. Nathan was filling them out with the kind of grin Steve Buscemi might have crossing names off a list with a tube of lipstick.

I ask him about it and he calmly starts explaining that he's "having trouble with the IRS."

I probe a little deeper since that in no way explains more than one check or envelope and he starts telling me about how last year during tax season he was in China for work so he started filling his taxes out early while at his parents' house. He owed a little but left before he could mail it in. Then he remembered while in China and broke through the firewall in order to pay it online. Unfortunately his parents, thinking he forget, wrote a check for him and mailed his taxes in too. So now his taxes would be paid twice. The IRS said don't worry about it, we'll cancel the check.

Well, it turns out that New York State IRS has a cancelled check fee of something like forty dollars and they sent Nathan a bill and penalty for the forty dollars.

That was it. That was the whole story. A forty dollar fee.

"Nathan, why do you have twenty checks on your desk?" I ask

cautiously.

"Oh, well after I explained to them what was wrong with the fee they didn't get it." So Nathan spent the next 4 weeks escalating the issue to the point that he got a case officer—a real, live human agent on the phone with a case number. Nathan started by asking for the agent to spell his name and politely to demonstrate that he was where he said he was by asking how the weather was and how the "drive in" had been that day. He then asked for his agent's manager, got their name and exchanged some pleasantries.

Nathan explained that his parents wrote the check but that he was the one being charged the fee. The agent explained that this was the policy of the IRS—"All cancelled checks will result in a forty dollar fee". The agent and Nathan went in rigorous compliant circles for hours exploring the rules. Nathan then calmly confirmed that:

1.) It is the policy of the IRS to allow just anyone to write a check on behalf of anyone else. "Yes sir that is fine. You just need to indicate the name and zip code of the account."

2.) It is the policy of the IRS to charge a forty dollar cancellation fee to the person whose account is indicated on the check. "Yes sir, that is the policy in New York State."

This means that, and I swear to God he actually asked the agent this hypothetical on the phone, "I could write a ten dollar check and indicate it's for the agent at 1234567 Schenectady, NY, and cancel it resulting in a forty dollar fee for you with absolutely no penalty or recourse to me?"

The equally compliant and rule-minded agent replied, "Yes sir, I guess you could."

So, that's what Nathan did.

And that's what he was doing with twenty checks on his desk and what he meant by "IRS trouble". He was following through . . . sending checks to the IRS addressed to pay the taxes of the agent and the agent's manager so Nathan could cancel them, causing the agent and his manager to owe the IRS a fee for each cancelled check. He was exploiting the same flaw in the system in which he was caught to essentially extort the IRS agents.

I laughed about this for weeks after, until about three weeks later when I'll be damned if he didn't receive a call from the IRS, a choice line of which was:

"Sir, we understand the point you've made. Please consider your fee waived and I hope we can put this behind us."

38

Posted by **DrRaveNinja**

Harass my daughter on Minecraft? You can't hide from me.

My daughter, who was about eight at the time, was *really* into the video game Minecraft (as most kids are these days). Desperately wanting to join the YouTube/Let's Play culture, I had installed some screen recording software for her that would let her make videos of the games she was playing so she could later upload them to YouTube.

One day I'm minding my own business when I hear her quietly sniffling at the computer. I asked her what was wrong, but she didn't want to tell me so I let it go, but decided to keep an eye on her. A few minutes later I discovered what was happening.

Someone was harassing not only her but also all the other kids playing on whatever server she was on. This kid was saying shit about how he was going to rape my eight year old daughter (she told him how old she was hoping he would stop), how he was going to hack into her IP to steal all her info and he was cursing profusely etc. By this time I had gotten my fiancé involved, and she was also obviously quite upset at what a little shit this kid was being. We realized that our daughter had been recording the entire incident, and a plan began to form.

I started by googling the kid's username. There were several hits immediately, the most interesting of which involved a page where he was publicly applying to be a mod for a server on Minecraft. I was able to learn a lot about this little piece of shit.

He claimed to be fifteen, liked hockey, used to live in Toronto but now lives in Florida. But the bombshell was his skype contact info; it was literally *firstname.lastname*. I know your name now, you little shit.

So I head over to Facebook and search for the name. Nothing. On a hunch I searched for just the last name, while narrowing my results to only the state of Florida. Several dozen hits, so I start combing through each one until I find what I was looking for: a middle aged man with the same last name, whose profile indicates he was born in Toronto and now lives in Florida. I found your dad you little shit.

I sent the dad a message on Facebook, asking if he had a son with the kid's name who goes by his username on Minecraft. Dad confirmed I had the right guy. So my wife begins telling the dad everything that little shit was saying to my daughter, and we sent him the recorded video as proof.

Radio silence for a few days.

Then we got the message back. The kid had his computer taken away from him for the entire summer, and had also been lying about his age (he was only eleven, I think). His parents were fucking livid with him, and he surely hated the next few months of his life.

No one fucks with my daughter.

(Editor's note: while reading this story for the first time on Reddit an advert for Minecraft was plastered on the right side of my screen. The same thing happened with our proof reader months later.
I love the internet.)

39

Posted by **Dwasifar**

Try to bully me, new boss? This will be your shortest job ever.

Back in the day, I worked as an independent IT consultant and was hired on along with another independent to subcontract on a team for a major consulting house. Everyone else on the team was a consulting house employee. The two of us were not supposed to tell the client that we weren't part of consulting house, but the client figured it out pretty quickly because we independents were doing most of the work while consulting house's code monkeys were busy filling out spreadsheets all day and going on team-building exercises.

The project ran past its initial deadline, and my contract expired. I stayed on a week-to-week basis as a professional courtesy to get the project finished, because I liked the client if not the team. Unfortunately the consulting house project manager was booked somewhere else for his next gig, and they brought in a new guy to replace him—David.

David flew in on a Monday morning to get the project handed off to him, and immediately started pissing on everything to mark his territory. He was derogatory and belittling to the team, and liked to raise his voice. I was working in my office (well, actually a closet with folding tables that I shared with three other team members) and didn't hear what he was saying out in the main room, but I could sure hear his tone.

Then he burst in to the "office" and demanded, "How are we doing *specific payroll-related conversion task?*"

I said, "We're using *program X.*" He waved his hand dismissively and scoffed. "That's stupid. *Program X* won't work for this. You need to do something else."

The other indie was in the room at the time, and she saw me coming up out of my chair. Later she told me she thought I was going to deck him. I knew he was full of shit because I wrote *program X.* It was custom code for this project, and he had no way of knowing what it would or wouldn't do. He was just trying to bully me and be the alpha dog.

I did not deck him. Instead, I went to the client's payroll manager, with whom I'd been working closely for months, and who was driving the client side of the project. I laid it on the line and said, "Look, I know you know I don't work for the consulting house. I'm here on an independent contract. That contract is up, and I've been working here week-to-week just to get you guys through."

She told me she was aware of this.

I nodded. "Okay. This new guy David is a bully and a blowhard, and I won't work with him. I have no contract at this point, and with him running the project I won't be back next week. I'm not asking you to do anything specific about it - just letting you know as a courtesy so you can plan to transition my work to someone else."

She sat back in her chair, thought a moment, and said, "Okay. Thanks for letting me know."

Two hours later David was removed from his new position.

The payroll manager, faced with losing the one technical guy on the team who actually knew what was going on with a very complicated payroll system, called the higher ups and said "We don't want this new guy, take him away."

The consulting house rearranged some things to keep the original project manager with the project.

The funniest part of the whole thing was that business had scheduled a "welcome" dinner for David at a posh steakhouse that evening. Rather than create the further embarrassment of cancelling the dinner, they actually went ahead with it as a "farewell" dinner for David, who had been on the project for less than one day. It was fun to watch him try to put on a brave face for that.

I stayed with the project to the end after that, and yes, they went live successfully.

40

Posted by **Johnny Provolone**

The time I ruined my high school teachers career and got her fired in the greatest way possible.

This story is widely known amongst my family and is constantly brought up and joked about in my group of friends even years later.

I was a senior in high school at the time and I had never been the brightest student. I was a solid C student and I had never received a detention or had any kind of bad student record. This is important because to this day, I still have no idea why the teacher treated me this way. The teacher, who we will name Mrs. Frank, had been a teacher there for more than a decade and was widely known by students for being a petty, heartless bitch though the administrators saw her as the golden child.

Mrs. Frank taught algebra, which was my worst subject, so naturally I had issues understanding the lessons and would ask questions frequently. For some, these questions are easily answered but to me it was rocket science.

Usually when someone asks a dumb question no one should address it. However in Mrs. Frank's case she would belittle me in front of everyone by saying things like "and here comes the slow boy again", "wow surprise, surprise. You don't understand it again" and "really? We have to go extra slow for you today don't we" Etc, etc.

I tried going to the administration about it before, but again she was considered the golden child. They would send someone in to examine her during class, she would act respectful and normal for one day and go back to being a bitch the next.

This goes on for about half the year until I've had enough. In my state you can record a conversation in someone's place of business without both party's consent so I went to the local RadioShack, bought a recorder and secretly recorded every insult she would throw at me. I would sometimes instigate to make up for the lost time.

Go ahead, feed the fire.

Fast forward to the end of the year and I'm sitting in Mrs. Frank's class when I ask a question. Her response, and I quoting because it's burned in to my brain. "I've been teaching here for over ten years and that was the single dumbest question I've ever heard come from anyone's mouth."

She continued the lesson without answering the question.

I calmly stood up, packed up my stuff and headed to the nurses office to dismiss myself from school (we were allowed to dismiss ourselves if we were eighteen).

I went home, compiled all of the brutal tapes into one glorious masterpiece and headed back the next day to show the administrators. I sat down with the principal and we listened to a couple of the insults before he stopped me. He wanted more witnesses present as well as Mrs. Franks. He told me we would meet the next day where I could show him and the rest of the administrators the full tape.

I walk into school the next morning being the most nervous I've ever been for anything. I was called down to the office where I met with some board directors, the local school police officer, the principal, the vice principal and Mrs. Frank.

What followed were some of the greatest minutes of my life.

I watched as the administrators went from fed up with being in another useless meeting to furious and speechless, some of them even keeping their mouths open for the duration of the tape. I also watched Mrs. Frank go from confident and stuck up to her realizing that she had fucked up beyond repair. She was publicly torching herself in front of the most important people from the district.

The tape ended and the administrators looked around in astonishment. The principal turns to me and says, "I think we have heard everything we need to, thank you," and I was quietly dismissed from the room.

The final time I saw Mrs. Frank was her leaving the room. I looked back and we made eye contact through her tear filled eyes as I gave the biggest, most evil smile.

I returned to class the next week and Mrs. Frank was nowhere to be found. The story spread quickly throughout the school and I was seen as a saint. I had successfully gotten her fired and made it almost impossible for Mrs. Frank to return to her teaching career as well as cut off most of her connections she had with other teachers in the school. I had ruined her financially because no school district in the area would hire her.

41

Posted by **Mcnew**

My manager was an awful person to me, but I got her fired in an embarrassing fashion.

Years ago, shortly after I graduated high school, I got a new job to support myself during college. The new gig was in a pet store and I was working in the department that sold the fish, aquariums, reptiles and birds. The store manager was an awesome guy who I will call Kurt. He was an old school guy - went to work, worked hard and went home. That's all he expected out of you as well.

The immediate manager over my department was this large snaggletooth witch of a woman I'll call Stephanie.

We got off to a bad start because she quickly found out that I knew more about reptiles than she does (Stephanie preferred the fish, whereas I had kept snakes for the past 4-5 years). Her ego couldn't handle a fresh employee not needing her guidance. From then on she was terrible to me, singling me out to clean the goldfish tanks and had the other employees cover sales every day I worked. She would say rude things to me such as "you are the weak link in my team" and "you are the reason I'm having problems in this department".

Fast forward about a year, my hours had been cut by about twenty five percent.

I asked the store manager what the deal was and he told me that our department had lost too much money between lack of sales and broken merchandise. This puzzled me but I didn't think much of it because everybody's hours were cut.

Simultaneously a few coworkers and I had noticed something strange— Stephanie had recently taken much more interest in the customers. She insisted on helping certain customers and sending us to do busy work while they were there. A customer came in one evening and was talking to us about "how nice Stephanie is".

Turns out Stephanie was breeding all of her own animals (dogs, turtles and mice) and selling them to customers she met through our store but not through the store. Not only was this taking business from us, our store had a couple corporate policies (we did not feed nor sell mice as live food for snakes, and we donated a lot of time and money to shelters and we condemned breeding dogs and cats for sale).

Stephanie was making money by selling animals to the customers all the while her department had hours cut for all of its employees. It didn't quite make sense how this was costing us so much money until one evening I thought I had figured it out.

Stephanie was an otherwise lazy woman, but when one of "her" customers came in she was by their side the whole time. I watched closely as she followed a customer around, helping them pick out a cart full of expensive aquarium decorations and terrarium supplies like lights and bulbs. I followed and wrote down every item she grabbed. I wanted to see where this went. She directed the customer to a register and went to check them out (she's lazy, and would never do this for any other customers). I noted the time and went back to work.

I later spoke to other cashiers about Stephanie checking customers out and they said that she only ever rang up certain customers and she acted weird when she did it. They suspected she was abusing coupons for them or applying hefty discounts. I got my coworkers to corroborate my story about the under the table animal sales and suspicious behavior and I went to talk to the owner Kurt.

I handed him a paper with about twenty items and the time written on it. "I think if you look up a transaction from register two at this time last night you will find a large discount applied to it. These are the items I would expect you to find on that transaction."

He was a bit puzzled and I explained everything to him. I told him I didn't want to make any accusations before because I wasn't sure, but after seeing her in action I was pretty sure something was going on. He thanked me and assured me he would look into it.

A couple weeks later I was at work and I noticed Kurt was standing near the door watching closely. It just so happens Stephanie was coming in for her shift right about that time. The second she walked through the door he called her over to his office. Waiting in his office was a regional manager from corporate.

He looked at the list I gave him and looked up transactions from the night before. He found one at the exact time I wrote but it only had about half of the items I listed – however every item that was on the receipt was on the list I gave him. This prompted him to watch her for a few weeks and in that time frame they found her to be taking "her customers" around shopping, personally taking them up to the register and scanning every other item and putting the expensive stuff into the cart without ringing it up.

In that time span she had given away over one thousand five hundred dollars in merchandise and he looked back at the logs we keep for broken merchandise that is written off and found an excessive amount of aquarium supplies and decorations that were signed off by her. It was something like a thousand percent more written off broken merchandise than was found at the same time last quarter.

All in all she was charged with stealing and defrauding the store of over three and a half thousand dollars in merchandise. It just so happened that Kurt had already arranged for police to meet them after firing her to escort her out.

I don't know if she went to jail, but I did watch her get walked out by police with about twenty employees staring along with me. I wish I could have said something, but I had to settle for her making eye contact with me as she walked out, to which I gave her a quick wink.

42

Posted by **Twilling8**

Thief tried to steal my car, accidentally filled it up with gas and brought it back to me instead

In the nineties my first car was a 1984 Jeep CJ7—a pretty sweet ride for a dirt poor teenager.

I was working midnight shifts at a gas station and loaned it to my brother who was taking a date to a party. I got a call around one in the morning from my brother who told me he left the keys in the Jeep and it was stolen.

I was devastated.

While still on the phone with my brother the thieves pulled my Jeep into my gas station to fill up on gas.

As luck would have it, the gas gauge on my Jeep was broken and always read "empty" and I worked at the only twenty four hour gas station in the area. I pressed the silent alarm and . . . proceeded to fill up my Jeep (it was a full service station).

When the thieves got out of the jeep I saw an opportunity to slip the key out of the ignition and into my pocket. They paid for the gas, then argued amongst each other who had the keys last. The delay was enough for the police to arrive.

I had to explain the story to the officer half a dozen times before he understood. The thieves had this stunned look of disbelief on their faces I'll never forget. The cops were belly-laughing telling the story to dispatch, all the while the thieves sat in cuffs in the back of the squad car.

The story made most of the major newspapers the following day.

43

Posted by **Plywood-**

Young and rude adults refuse to pay for public transport, but oooh sweet revenge at the end of the day.

I work as a train driver, piloting smaller trains mostly out on the countryside and people are generally nice and well behaved. Of course, there are also the alcoholics, drug addicts and general weirdoes that uses public transport—and some people that just live to be a pain in the ass.

This was a few years ago, while we were traveling in the late afternoon and my conductor storms into the drivers cabin, angry and annoyed. "We have two rude, good-for-nothing guys onboard and they're such assholes!"

"What did they do?" I ask.

"They have no tickets, refused to pay, just laughed up in my face and then said 'what are you gonna do about it?'"

"Well, should I help you throw them off at the next stop?"

"We can't because they're just traveling one station so they're getting off at the next stop!" She complains. "Damn smug guys with their 'what are you gonna do about it?' Honestly."

We're both angry so I let the conductor rant and let off some more steam.

Next stop comes and the guys get off while the conductor angrily gestures at them. "That's the two."

We continue the remaining short journey and have a break at the end station. Some hours later the train then goes back. Since it's on the countryside and it's late evening on a weekend the train is almost empty on the way back. The conductor knows where every passenger on board is getting off and she's up at front with me, chatting and all is fine again.

Until we approach the station where we let those guys off.

We see two people standing there. It. Is. Them. My conductor beside me shines up like a damn sun.

With the biggest smile on her face she says, "Do not stop."

I'm just laughing, slowing down the train but not stopping. When we pass them my conductor opens the window, waves and says loud and happily, "This is what I'm going to do about it!"

The guys are just staring at her with their jaws on the ground when we drive past them, laughing all the way to our home station.

Ours was the last train for the day.

We encountered these guys again a few weeks later, and these guys did not learn the first time.

They apparently got on at the same station like last time but we didn't notice them. They had plans to travel further than last time but when the conductor went out to check the tickets she spots them, recognize them and speaks loudly so the other travelers can hear. "Ooh, are you able to pay for your tickets today?"

They just fidgeted before saying, "No, we ain't got no money."

"Well, ain't that a shame!" the conductor says gleefully. "Guess you have to get off at the next stop!"

"What the hell," one complains. "Can't you be nice and let us be? What the fuck are we gonna do at that shitty station?"

"Guys, I don't give a damn. You're getting off this train and can walk to the next station, and I'm calling the train behind us so they won't pick you up either."

They got off, the other train called us later because they saw the guys walking on a forest path along the railway track.

And we haven't seen these guys since.

44

Posted by **AtelierVieuxPont**

Credit card skimmer gets what he bought with my card...and a bit extra

This story starts off on a slightly less humorous note—a few days ago I was on the unfortunate end of credit card fraud.

The fraudster's decided to take my credit card information and purchase a thousand dollars' worth of car parts from Philly and have it sent across the border to the city I currently live in, Vancouver, Canada.

Normally this is where the story ends. Sometimes they get away with it, sometimes they don't but either way my card is replaced and I continue on living my life. This however, is where the fun starts happening.

I got a call this morning about a DHL shipment entering the country that required customs to be paid. Knowing I haven't shipped anything with DHL in forever I quickly come to the realization that it must be the fraudster's shipping their goods here.

It can't be I thought. Who in their right mind would use a stolen credit card to order something to their own house in the city the owner of the card lives.

After a brief chat with DHL about the customs fees I will not be paying I manage to obtain the address the package was being sent to. I hummed and hawed about it but eventually decided the best thing to do was call the local police department and let them know what was up.

I told the officer all about the situation—that unfortunately I did not know what car the parts were for and that I hope this info helps them somehow in the future. He tells me that the chances are slim but he will swing by the house (it's literally fifteen minutes from my own) just to see if anything weird is going on and follow up with me if he needs to. I thank him and go on with my work day.

About an hour later I get a call from the same officer, obviously excited. "Hi, it's Officer Jones. You will never guess what just happened. I was following up on the report and drove by the house. I decided to go knock on the door just to see if anyone was home and ask them a couple questions. A man opened the door and as we were talking DHL drove up to deliver the package. Yes that's right, the exact package we had been discussing.

"The delivery driver walks up to the door and says 'Hi, is AtelierVieuxPont here?' to which the man replies 'Oh yeah, he's just downstairs."

You can imagine my surprise!

"That's pretty funny," the officer continues to tell me. "Because I just got off the phone with him and I know for a fact he doesn't live here."

The guy looked the officer dead in the face and says, "Oh whatever, the package is paid for."

The officer chuckled and turned to the DHL driver to tell him he should leave because he needed to make an arrest.

"I'm calling you while I'm driving back to the precinct," the officer tells me. "Thought it might brighten your day!"

I still cannot believe that they caught the guy, but thought it was a story that was too good not to share.

45

Posted by **Meschugena**

Contractor abandons project mid-way, resulting in damages. Tries to go off the grid. But I found him and now he's paying me every penny.

This is a bit of a long one so I will try to keep some details out that aren't necessary to the story. It takes place over the course of a year.

The story begins with my needing to hire a contractor to repair damage to a pole barn that I was constructing on our property. The structure was partially done when a storm hit and the structure had substantial damage. We bid a few contractors and the guy that seemed to be the best one (who was actually a referral from a friend) signed a contract and he started work within a week.

We had also signed with him to complete the structure after the insurance portion was completed because his crew could do this much more efficiently and a better job than we could do ourselves (which is what we were originally doing).

His crew completes the insurance portion of the job, but then abandons the project just before starting the rest of it.

No call, no email, nothing.

I called and texted—not one of my contact points was ever returned. At this point it was late December, and we thought maybe he and his crew had holiday plans but would resume right after. Then another windstorm hit and his crew hadn't braced the partially-completed structure correctly . . . and it almost collapsed again.

I tried for two weeks to find him. I even drove out to the address on the contract we signed, which ended up being a house on a rural road the next town over. Seeing his car there I knocked on the door. No one answered. I stopped by this house several different times trying to catch him. The last few times his car was no longer there but the work truck of another company was.

Wanting to know if he owned the house I pulled up the tax records for it in the county it was in. The name on the house was not registered to him. It sounded like he rented or at least was staying with a friend. The company info on the truck was registered to someone unrelated and not on the tax records either. The tax records showed that the actual taxpayer of the property lived elsewhere.

Here where I live, the property owner's name is listed and if they do not actually live at that property (such as using it for an investment) their address that would have the actual tax bill sent to is also on there.

With that knowledge I pulled the court records for him to see if maybe he had been recently arrested or if there was any other info. What I found was about thirty years of driving offenses, including a lot of drunk driving charges and other records. At this point I figured he was long gone and because I hadn't paid out any money to him for work that was not complete I would just move on.

At least until the structural engineer I hired to assess the damage to the work that was done stated that the structure had to be started over where the contractor had worked and the building materials that the contractor had left scattered around the jobsite were also unusable due to being left improperly stored. I had hoped that the structure could just be pulled back into place and re-secured but I was told this is not the case.

And so began the bigger drama and my determination to find him.

So far his negligence has cost me a thousand two hundred dollars for a structural engineer's opinion (our insurance company paid for a second opinion because they didn't like what ours had said), two and a half thousand for insurance deductibles to the newest contractor hired to repair the exact damage that happened three months prior and seven thousand in materials that his insurance company refused to cover or pay for. My insurance policy on the project did not want to cover it either.

The adjuster for his insurance company said that he was able to locate the contractor but refused to give up any information for him directly. That and the fact that the project wasn't finished was a detriment to my farm and boarding business because two of my pastures that were connected to where the building was sitting couldn't be used. This limited my ability to use natural pasture grass in summer months by rotating pastures for each herd, and had to purchase hay which gets quite expensive.

By the time the building was completed and I could get my pastures back to normal I had losses of over fourteen thousand dollars. Because I didn't know where he now lived I used the only address I had for him to file for small claims court, which here has a limit of fifteen thousand. The court documents I served came back undeliverable. This meant that I was kind of stuck because a court date cannot be scheduled until all parties are properly served.

But how do I find an address for someone who doesn't seem to register to any particular address directly?

Time was still on my side as this was still early-mid last year. I kept a watch on social media for anything with his name, which was a very unique one. If there was another man with the same name within this state, within even the same metro area, it was unlikely because of how unique the name was.

Then one day this past fall, after google searching the name again, there it was - his Facebook page. His name hadn't shown up before with several searches. Not sure why this was the case. Even better all his settings were set to public. I could see everything he wrote about, including his recent commitment to stay sober earlier in 2017 (just after he abandoned my project) and . . . his employer's name!

He had posted a pic of him on a jobsite and someone asked where he worked now. He named the place. One quick google search and voila! I got an address to serve him court papers to. I re-filed with the new-found address, but I still needed a home address to enforce the judgement once I won the case.

So what did I do?

Seeing that he was listed as "single" on his page I used a fake Facebook profile that I originally had in use to test various features I enable on pages that I start up under my real profile to serve another purpose - getting this guy to give me all the information I needed by playing on his being middle aged and single.

To create my alter ego I found a website of a cute blonde lady in her forties (so as to not be too young for him, since he was around mid-forties himself) and just yanked pictures. I only set one to the profile photo, and would use the rest if he asked for more. I changed all the pictures in the profile to look like it was a typical page of the average mid-forty's female.

Holy crap did this work . . . and it worked so well.

I used some information I found on his page to strike up a conversation about stuff stolen out of his work truck in the alley behind his house (big clue!) and it was reported to the city police department (he named the city, so another big clue). Using this information, and telling him I had grown up in the same area, I got him to give me a general area where he lived - keeping conversation cool like "is the pizza joint still there? They've been around forever" so he wouldn't get suspicious.

Thank goodness for Google Maps giving me a better idea of that area so I could talk about it like I did in fact grow up there. In reality, I have only ever been in that city twice and other times drove through on the way to somewhere else.

I was able to narrow down the area he talked about, and using that info I pulled the police report records from that city. There were three reports done within the same area on that same day he got reported. From there I pulled the county tax records to see who owned the houses. I found three houses within that area that could possibly be rentals since the owner name and taxpayer billing address did not match. This could be a long-shot to find the person, but I didn't have anything to lose by searching.

Just as I was about to call the homeowners to see if anyone by the name of the contractor rented from them he posts some info on his page that made the calls completely unnecessary - the name of his roommate in a status update, who I then check out the profile of. The profile lists the roommate's landscaping business. A quick google search of that business name and bingo, his state business registration address matched one of the three addresses I suspected to be the rental house.

Now I had his home address.

Fast forward to the court date - he didn't show up, which I suspected he wouldn't so I got default judgement. Between serving him papers and the court date passing the Facebook profile I was using to talk to him was helpful in getting info out of him about his life, job situation, how much he made per hour (thanks to me feigning knowledge about what construction trades paid) and the fact that he was looking at changing employers. He even told me the name of that employer. So I was armed with info should he decide to not work with me.

He played right into my hands.

Once I got the official judgement from the small claims court win I decided to contact him myself on Facebook using messenger. I sat down and wrote out a whole paragraph to him, first typing it on Word so that I could print it out and edit it and had my husband read it as well.

I wrote that while I was angry at him, I was going to give him one chance to work a deal with me rather than using our state department of revenue play collection officer for me. I hate dealing with our state department of revenue - they make the IRS look like Sunday school teachers. But if it came down to that I would, and they would start garnishing his wages. Here they take a quarter of each paycheck after taxes and have the person's employer do it for them then send it to me. I hate letting the state be the middle-man because they just complicate things.

I told him straight out that if he refused to work with me directly, I would go to that extreme. I told him that I know he's an addict and has had struggles in the past. I told him that knowing he has had struggles I was willing to work with him directly and give him an opportunity to offer a monthly payment amount that works for him and his budget, rather than have the state decide the amount for him.

He replied, agreed, signed (and had notarized) a monthly payment agreement, complete with a list of manual labor tasks that he could use in place of a payment or two to help with some projects on my farm.

So far so good and it is nice having that payment show up every month.

(Editor's note: The lengths to which the author went to get justice are both impressive and mind boggling, so it's evening more commendable that after all that there was still compassion left to make a deal. Much respect.)

46

Posted by **somehugefrigginguy**

New asshole in a peacefull neighborhood learns his lesson

I live in a quiet little town in the Midwestern United States. My house is the last house at the end of a sleepy dead-end road. A new guy moves in next door, let's call him Richard.

He was probably one of those guys who was so popular in high school that he thought he had it made without doing any work and tried to spend the rest of his life living off being "the cool guy". The type of guy who drives a lifted truck and a motorcycle. Now don't get me wrong, I ride motorcycles myself. What I don't do is sit in my driveway at two AM and rev my engine.

There's a bit of a downhill slope from the middle of the street to our houses at the end, and Richard likes to race down this hill, then lock his brakes and "drift" into his driveway. The first winter after he moved in I noticed that my mailbox has been crushed and there's fresh tire tracks in the snow leading down the street, over my mailbox and into his driveway.

A few days later I see Richard standing outside and ask him about the mailbox. He denies the entire thing, says he doesn't know what happened to my mailbox and that it must've been a delivery guy or something. I figure whatever and fix my mailbox.

A few months later the same thing happens again. I fix my mailbox and move on. Sometime later, this happens yet again. This time I'm pretty pissed.

I talked to my cousin who's a commercial welder and had him make me a mailbox out of some scrap quarter-inch steel plate which was mounted on a length of old railroad track for its post. A little bit of glue and some cedar shingles and you'd never know it wasn't a typical wooden mailbox. Also, the railroad track "post" was sunk in concrete four feet into the ground.

For the next several weeks I waited with anticipation every time I heard his truck roaring down the street, but nothing. Until about five months later when I heard his truck, then a crash.

By this time I had forgotten about my mailbox and thought for sure he'd struck another car. I ran out to the street to see if anyone needed help and there was his truck broadside against my mailbox, all smashed up.

He saw me walk up and started yelling about how I had destroyed his truck and he'd make me pay. He called the cops.

An officer showed up to take his report and Richard pointed out how my mailbox had been specifically designed to destroy his truck. I have to admit, I got nervous at this point. The cop looked around at the truck and the construction of the mailbox, then turned back to us and asked me if I'd had trouble with my mailbox before.

I explained how it has been smashed several times in the past year.

"It's pretty clear what happened here," the cop replied. "This is an obvious case of wanton destruction of property."

My heart sunk to the ground and Richard got a smug look on his face, but then cop turns to Richard and add, "I'm going to issue a citation for this, as well as reckless driving".

You should have seen Richard's face at this point. He was boiling with rage as the cop wrote him two tickets and told him he needed to pay for the repair of the damaged wood on my mailbox (the metal was fine, he hadn't even tilted it but the wood camouflage had broken off).

47

Posted by **NewNameNoah**

Employer screwed me over, I screwed him back with help from the FBI.

It was the early nineties and I worked for a telemarketing company in Logan, UT. I was employed for two full days when I came to the conclusion that we were just scamming old people out of their money using grossly unethical methods.

I quit after my second day of work and when I received my paycheck I noticed that I was paid minimum wage instead of the ten dollars per hour I was promised when they hired me so I went back to complain.

"You didn't finish the ninety day probationary period so you only get minimum wage," the office manager told me.

Bullshit.

They never said anything about a probationary period in training and I know it wasn't in the contract I signed upon hire (yeah, I actually read it before signing it). As the office manager opened the door to have me leave he had some choice words for me.

"See ya, wouldn't wanna be ya."

I was fuming.

I called the city offices and discovered that the telemarketing company didn't have a business license and reported them. Less than an hour later I watched as the police showed up and told them they would have to shut down operations until they had a business license.

It took 'em two weeks.

When they were back in business I used an elaborate scheme to get myself on their call list and recorded several of their employee's efforts to sell me their crap (it was Utah and legal to record the calls). I knew what they were doing wasn't just unethical, it was illegal.

Not only did I report it to a local news station who had their consumer reporter do a two part story on the scummy company but I also reported them to the FBI.

The owner of the company was one of the two hundred plus people that was arrested by the FBI in a nationwide sting of dishonest telemarketing companies. The FBI called it "Operation Disconnect".

"See ya, wouldn't wanna be ya."

Ha!

48

Posted by **Saria19**

Group attempted to cut me out after I did about 60% of the work. They failed.

This happened about twelve years ago while I was studying Aeronautical Engineering. Due to some money-grubbing legislation tactics, most who have gone to college knew about the unnecessary courses that are tacked onto the degrees in order to graduate. One of those courses for my degree was a business class (seriously, you'd think these guys would understand that most Engineers don't do the business side of things). Thankfully, we had a teacher who was understanding of the fact that many of us in the class were bored out of our minds.

I'll admit to having always been a nerd who loved making good grades. If I don't understand something, I run at it hard to try to change that. This class stumped me for quite some time and then a nightmare of a project was announced—one worth half of our grades.

The school was a small one, the class a little more than thirty people and I was assigned to work with three students I knew from other classes. We had problems straight away.

Two of the people remembered me from a Calculus class that they barely passed as the person who sailed easily through and decided to dump their portion of the work on me straight away, knowing I wouldn't allow myself to fail. They were right.

At first my other group member tried to pick up the slack as well, pulling hard to do a difficult project in a subject we barely understood. I'll admit she was a trouper. Unfortunately, she was also someone easily manipulated and our two slacking group members began applying pressure during the semester for her to take the work and allow them to present it.

The day of the project finally comes and I'm sick as a dog, pretty much quarantined in the clinic due to bronchitis. I managed to send a message to the teacher. The two slackers manage to wrangle the presentation from the girl who worked with me and presented it to the class, declaring that they had done all of the work and I was skipping class because they had told me that they were going to tell the teacher what happened.

My initial grade was an F. I was beyond pissed until I realized something important—part of the project involved a written report, of which, I held the only copy since I was the one who typed it up.

Cue the revenge.

I went to the teacher privately with my notes and the report in order to get the grade I earned and to get him in on the plot. He agreed since it seemed fun and he planned to fail them anyway for academic dishonesty. Publicly, there was no report.

The classmates that had attempted to take all the credit began to approach me, first demanding the report. Most of the time, my response was "But I didn't do any work!" in a sickly sweet voice.

Next they attempted to act all buddy-buddy, trying to convince me that it had all been a joke and promising that they'd tell the professor that I had done some work, giving me some credit so that I had the possibility to pass. This was met with stony silence on most occasions before I told them that I'd rather fail than let them pass.

Things escalated after that to include the door of my dorm room being rapped on at odd hours of the night, shoving and them stealing my backpack and notebooks in order to try to find the report themselves. One of them even asked my roommate to let them search for a report I had written and forgotten for our group (didn't have her as my roommate the following semester).

Things finally came to a head on the last week of classes. I had held out on them for a month, not telling any of my group mates what I had done and enough time had elapsed that even if they were to turn in the report now it would be so late that they'd still have failed. They hadn't even attempted to do the report themselves and the girl who had worked with me was in hysterics over the very real possibility of failing the class. It was what the teacher and I had been waiting for and he finally decided to return the reports.

The two slackers glared daggers at me as the teacher returned the report of every other group in the class before stopping in front of them. He was holding what looked to be one extra report and they were immediately looking hopeful. He set a single sheet of paper on one of their desks before moving to the desk of the girl who had worked along with me and set the report on her desk.

"I had to dock some points for dishonesty, but you and your partner did decently," he stated before moving on.

My partner realized what I had done. We only got an eighty two on our project, but it was far better than the zero that our ex-group mates received.

I had been carefully documenting the harassment that the two slackers had put me through and ensured several witnesses saw some of what they did. Two days after being informed that they were failing, the pair had a new problem—I gave the evidence to the administration of our school and the teacher reported the academic dishonesty. The administration did a bit more digging and found that the pair had been making trouble for some time and a number of students reported similar problems of having their work stolen.

The slackers were expelled.

49

Posted by **ThomasofHookton**

Re-use unfinished soups for the next customer? Loose your restaurant.

This revenge story happened in the nineties when I was working after school as a line cook and chef's assistant at a Chinese restaurant. The place specialized in noodle soups, with the main attraction being our soup stock. The owner used a much revered, passed down family recipe. It consisted of freshly cracked pork bones, fresh spices and fresh vegetables all kept at a rolling boil for over twelve hours. It had to be started the night before and the owner was very particular about the soup stock.

If it ran out, then it ran out. He refused to "cheat" as some places do by adding water or powdered stock.

The owner himself was this really awesome, old Chinese gentleman. He had some incredible stories. For example, he enlisted into the Kuo Ming Tang (Chinese Republic) Army in the forties and worked as a chef for KMT officers during WWII. He told us about how one time his division's HQ was over run, and he had to escape on a push bike ahead of the advancing Japanese Army. Eventually, when the Chinese Communist Party took over in the fifties he was assigned to a steel factory to work for the rest of his life.

He got out and eventually made his way to the U.S. as an asylum seeker. I digress, but my point is that he was an awesome guy and was a genuinely kind and considerate boss. He always made sure his employees were fed before the evening shift and let me study during quiet nights.

His son on the other hand, was a real piece of shit.

This guy dropped out of college (his parents saved up for him to study medicine) after two years. He floated in and out of jobs but mostly stayed unemployed, living with his parents and using their money to well into his mid-thirties. He eventually started working at the restaurant, nominally as the front of house manager but in reality did nothing but watch TV and take naps.

While I was only a line cook, the old man and I got along really well. He trusted me and would routinely get me to make the soup stock the night before under his supervision.

Sadly, the old man died after my fifth year working there. That's when the son took over (the mother had passed years ago).

The son had zero cooking experience but decided to take over as the chef. He didn't like the idea of putting the soup on overnight (waste of gas) and instead got me to do the prep the night before and then would just switch the pot on himself in the morning.

He would also routinely add plain water to the soup when it got low so he could continue selling noodle soups. The most incredible, disgusting thing however, was he got the wait staff to throw customer's unfinished soups back into the stock pot for reuse. When I confronted him about it he told me that it was no problem as the heat killed any germs and threatened to fire me if I said anything.

Not surprisingly customers started leaving as the food quality degraded. This caused the son to panic and cut even more costs. He fired most of the old staff and thus overworked the remaining. He couldn't fire me because I was the only one left who knew how to do the soup. Also he stopped using quality ingredients and started to buy cheap, pre-packaged stuff in order to reduce my prep work hours.

After a few months of this I got sick of his crap. As I was about to start college myself I told him that I was giving him my notice. Of course he took this poorly and told me that I was a loser. He then told me not to bother coming in tomorrow, but I was to spend the remainder of my shift showing a recent hire how to do my job, stating that he would not issue my last check if I didn't complete a thorough hand over.

I laughed in his face and walked out on the spot, not bothering to chase up my last check.

As a parting gift I sent an email to our local Food Safety Board, informing them of the poor sanitary practice of reusing left over soups. I helpfully also enclosed a few photos that I had sneakily taken of the practice. The board sent inspectors the very next day and closed the restaurant (there were other issues such as unhygienic bathrooms, uncleaned eating utensils).

He was issued a massive fine and a list of undertakings to carry out before it could be re-opened. The restaurant remained closed and was eventually sold. I didn't bother chasing up what happened to the son but I hope he has learnt his lesson and done something productive with his life.

50

Posted by **Viper896**

Oh, it's not your job? It is now.

My dad was a mechanic for twenty plus years, and for as long as I can remember, I drove him nuts because I would go around the house with a screw driver he left out and take everything apart because I wanted to see how it worked.

As I grew older I developed an affinity towards computers and electronics, which led me to be "that kid" in high school who changed his grades, crashed the school districts servers and used the ***net send*** command with great success. I would spend my weekends either with my grandparents and uncle working on science projects or dragging my dad outside to help me fix my car (which consisted of him telling me that he would help once I got it taken apart). Those "figure it out" lessons were probably the greatest gift he could've given me.

I joined the U.S. Army in March of 2004 and went into communications, "commo" for short, (25U) where I managed to go from PVT (E1) when I joined to SGT (E5) by the time I returned from my deployment at the beginning of 2007.

After returning home I was subsequently transferred from a Light Infantry Unit (walking everywhere) to a Mechanized Infantry Unit (riding in an armored vehicle everywhere). I was placed in charge of the Battalion Commo Shop because the current person running the commo shop was scheduled to retire in a few months and I was the only other NCO. This is where things got interesting.

As anyone else that was in the U.S. Army can attest to, every Monday is "motor pool maintenance", which essentially means—go make sure all the tanks, Bradley Fighting Vehicles (BFV) or anything else with a motor works the way it should. This included testing all the radios and communication equipment as well. If it didn't work, we filled out the maintenance forms with the correct shop and have them fix it.

All the issues would later be consolidated into a report that the leadership team would review. If a vehicle was on that report, the leadership team wanted to know why it wasn't fixed. I ran my shop using the same approach my dad taught me, which was "figure it out" and don't come to me with a problem unless you have a solution.

One Monday morning, shortly after taking charge of the commo shop, one of my soldiers came to me with a problem he couldn't figure out and asked if I could come help him. I agreed and followed him over to the BFV that was giving him problems. After a few hours of troubleshooting we finally traced the problem to the BFV's slip ring. We double and triple checked that indeed was the problem because slip rings in general have a low failure rate and it wasn't something we could fix on our own. It required help from the mechanics because the slip ring required taking apart the interior of the BFV turret to actually get to it.

I went to the mechanics to get their help so we could fix the problem. This is when I learned the mechanics didn't like the commo shop. I was essentially told by the motor chief to F-off and that the slip ring is a commo issue. It's the commo shop's job to fix it—not theirs.

I was pissed at the response and tried to insist we needed his help. However, I was promptly shut down and told to pound sand. At this point, I was beyond pissed.

I tried the official way, I even swallowed my pride and asked him nicely. Both times I was shit on. So I decided I was going to play Global Thermonuclear War and teach him a lesson that neither he nor anyone else in his shop would forget.

I went to my guys and told them I would be back in about an hour or two because I needed to run home and grab some stuff. When I got home, I went directly for the garage and started packing all the wrenches, impacts and sockets that I could fit into my portable toolbox. I also loaded up the portable air compressor and any extension cords I could find and made my way back to the motor pool.

Once I got back I had my guys locate every extension cord they could find around the office, because I could only find one in my garage, and help me run power out to the BFV that we were going to have to fix ourselves. Meanwhile, I also had two of the guys run to the H.Q. and find me two of largest empty coffee cans they could find. I ended up having to tell them twice because the first time they thought I was joking . . . they couldn't understand why I needed a coffee can of all things.

When they returned with coffee cans I had everything in place—power, compressed air, tools and a place to neatly put all of the bolts, nuts and washers I was about to remove.

Under normal circumstances I would only remove the things that absolutely had to be removed—the fewer things to put back together, the better. But these weren't normal circumstances, and I had absolutely no intention of putting anything back together.

It was about lunch time and I decided my way of fixing this issue probably wasn't the best example to set for my team, so I sent them to lunch and told them I would handle this issue so they could focus on the other vehicles when they got back.

For the next few hours I proceeded to dismantle every single bolt I could find.

I removed seats, interior plates, shelves—pretty much anything that wasn't electrical or commo related got removed. I would then place all of the newly removed hardware in the coffee cans. By the time I reached the turret I had filled up both coffee cans with nuts, bolts and washers so I had to go find something else to start putting this stuff in. Luckily we had Zip-Lock bags by the dozen laying around the office. I grabbed a couple of those and went back to having fun taking apart the BFV.

I finally reached the slip ring and managed to luck out. I didn't have to replace the slip ring after all!

Turns out the mechanics didn't install one of the cable mounts and one of the commo cables got snagged and subsequently cut. It probably took me less than fifteen minutes at that point to replace the cable and missing cable mount (of course the fact that I completely removed everything in the way helped because now I didn't have to fish the cable through anything).

Once I replaced the cable and made sure all of the other commo equipment worked, I figured while I had everything taken apart it would be much easier to fix any other problems they might have been having. All commo systems checked out, my job was done.

Everything that I had taken out of the BFV was then gently and neatly stacked in the interior of the BFV. I put the lids on the coffee cans, zipped up the bags, pulled out my trusty sharpie and wrote "bolts" on each of them.

After everything was tidied up I went off to find the owner of the BFV and let him know his commo issue was fixed, but he should probably have a mechanic look at his BFV because I had to disassemble some (and by some I meant "most") of the vehicle in order to get to the part I needed to replace and I couldn't remember how everything went back together.

I stared out of my office window for the rest of the day waiting for the mechanics to get around to looking at the BFV. I still remember the reaction of the motor chief when he looked inside that vehicle. If I didn't know any better, I could have sworn his head rotated around three times and damn near popped off. His reaction was absolutely priceless.

I knew he was about to storm into my shop in a fit of rage, so I got up and decided it was probably best to meet him outside in motor pool. As soon as I reached earshot distance he started screaming and demanding I put the vehicle back the way I found it. However, I was having none of that.

I simply shook my head. "It's a 'mechanical issue' now, and that's not my job. I asked for your help in the beginning and was told no because it wasn't your job. I'm just a commo guy. I didn't know what needed to be removed to fix the commo issue in the slip ring, so I removed everything. If someone from your team would have been there, I think this whole misunderstanding could have been avoided."

That vehicle remained on the weekly report for the next three weeks while they figured out what bolts went where.

However, after that incident I was never told "It's not my job" ever again and the mechanics were more than willing to help me fix any issues that came up. By the time I left the unit we ended up starting to cross train each other's team members so we could fix things faster as they came up.

51

Posted by **greyspot00**

Downstairs neighbors wouldn't turn down "music," nuked them from orbit.

I moved out on my own in 2013 and moved into an old house converted into a two floor apartment, directly across from my future in-laws.

The downstairs neighbors were loud. *Blaring* music at all hours (yes, all of the hours), wouldn't cut the grass or take out the trash on our shared schedule. Crappy neighbors, but never bothered me directly. The guy was pretty chill when sober and would turn the music down a little when I texted him. He was okay until his girlfriend moved in. Now add shouting matches to the mix, and all of the sudden my requests to turn down the music makes him turn it up.

Yet I can barely walk on my super-thin floor without her banging on the ceiling with a broom.

I was okay since I am heavy sleeper and could sleep through anything. My wife moved in, and I quickly found out that she is quite the opposite. Fan on turned at a certain angle in the doorway of the bathroom, door closed half way, blackout curtains with them taped to the wall so zero light comes through, zero sounds other than the fan—you get the idea.

I told her that we can't expect them to remain silent when she's ready for bed, we need to be reasonable, but the wall rattling music needs to stop during the night. She hated it during the day, but I told her there's nothing we can do then so she would go to her parent's house a lot during the day.

I talked to neighbor-guy.

"Yeah man that's cool," was his response, but it turns out the girlfriend wasn't having it and his attitude then changed to "yeah, well it's our house so you can go F yourself if you think you can tell us what to do and you can move out if you don't like it."

Something definitely had to change once she was pregnant, and then the baby came.

So I did the only thing I could do. I fought fire with fire, and *maliciously complied* with the law to the T.

I could only report them for noise after eleven PM. I now forget the morning hour when the noise could start, but I believe it was nine AM.

My dad has these huge old concert speakers in his garage. Professional grade, black leather bound, five feet tall and three feet wide plus a pretty nice, vintage stereo/amp.

He has two, but my apartment was so small I sadly only had room for one. We replaced our coffee table with this thing, laid face down onto our thin office carpet.

Tired of his crap tunes, I tested this Geneva Convention breaking device when they weren't home.

Holy cow.

I had to take everything down from tables, counters and shelves because they would shake off. I prepared audio files to feed the stereo. I was giddy like a kid with a new Christmas toy. I turned it on when I left for work and got my wife up to send her to her parents. I came home from work and hung out at her parents until it was close to bed time.

They resisted for three days.

On day two, I found a pile of manure on my doorstep, but it didn't faze me.

I cycled between sine/saw/square waves in clashing chords, marching music (Washington Post March on loop), preaching clips (they weren't just atheist, but outspoken anti-Christian, so it was a must), the most stupid songs you could think of (the Captain Planet theme song, Chicken Dance, etc).

The poor old house rattled in ways I didn't think possible. The vibrations from the sine wave would make your vision blur.

I eventually got a text from him that read "sorry man you can stop now."

I did not.

He needed a few more days to let it sink in. Plus, I had so much fun putting it together. They complained to the police and the landlord. There was nothing they could do since I wasn't doing anything wrong.

I didn't even hear music during the time of peace to follow. It was so quiet.

They would build up their courage and try again every few weeks when I wasn't home, but my wife was. I then showed her how to tame the beast so she could let it loose while I was away.

I had to give them a spanking every now and then, but they learned. They were so happy when we moved out.

52

someone stole 25k from me, it ended costing him half a million dollars

I was married to a very OCD and pragmatic man. For example—for him, a big romantic gesture, had been to leave me alone for twenty four hours at the hospital right after I had our son, so he could go pay bills and mow the lawn.

Twenty years later I do understand he really did express love this way. But that's another story.

I was in dire need of physical contacts because he'd never touched me, unless he wanted (very bland) sex, and also never ever kissed me. The story is not about him, it's only a preamble.

So I divorced him, not just for what's above mind you—I felt alone and unloved in this relationship. I just wrote about it to explain the state of mind I was in when I met this other person that we'll call Peter.

Peter was the total opposite.

He was very in tune with his emotions, was very, very intense (this will be important later). He really expressed love like I *thought* I needed. On our first date, the waitress asked how long we had been together since he was so into me and touching me.

He made me feel amazing. He had a huge house and a rather flashy lifestyle, so I assumed he was really well off. He told me he owned a car wash and a phone marketing company.

Fast forward a bit. At this point we had been dating for about a year, and he had just asked me (and my son) to move in with him. I wasn't one hundred percent sure, but he prepared the room for my son nonetheless.

As I started spending more time in his house (still keeping mine) I also started to see strange behavior. He'd be up all night, but sleep all day. I also overheard a few phone calls where he was telling people they owed money and needed to pay but the conversations didn't fit with a carwash or phone marketing business.

At some point he told me he was having money problems. Apparently huge clients were late in paying and that is was jeopardizing his house payments. So, I, stupid me, offered to help. I'm missing a part of this story because it started as me offering help with the house since we were there a lot (still had my house though) but it ended up with me lending him twenty five grand.

I cannot for the life of me remember that progression.

The loan was supposed to be for three weeks he said. I'd have it all back in three weeks. Three weeks . . .

That money came from my retirement savings/son's college money, so I had to pay a fine to access it. It's also money that took me ten years to put aside. That money was very important to me.

During those three weeks I went out to have drinks with my friends . . . and found him on a date with another woman. I saw him French kissing another woman . . . I said nothing, went to his house, packed my shit and left.

I thought he'd be an adult and would still reimburse the money the end of this three weeks.

Big mistake.

Someone I knew told me he was glad I left and proceeded to tell me about him. He said Peter was a junky, hooked on GHB, hence why he was so intense and so into his emotions. That also explained the erratic sleep patterns but the final blow was when he told me Peter was also a con man.

A "Specialist" in defrauding older people by phone, his so-called "phone marketing company".

In the beginning, I wasn't sure I believed it but then bits of what I had overheard in the last year started to make sense. I realized it was all true. Back to this later.

I tried getting my money back many different ways. None worked.

I was at the end of my rope, and since it was in my years post-divorce (and right after the 2008-2009 economic crash as well) I was poor as hell.

So this is what I did.

Previously he had given me access to pay bills online (not to his bank accounts, but to his emails) so I was able to investigate *all* his accounts with the same password. I printed and screenshotted every little bit of information relating to money.

I found proof that he was indeed scamming people and found the people he "worked" with and even the name of the person at the bank who facilitated the money transfer. I found out he was an organized criminal. I also found out he did this between the two countries. I started preparing strike one:

I printed his face and the face of everyone working for/with him (from their online profiles) in defrauding people and left hundreds of flyers in his neighborhood. I also called the hotline for financial crime prevention in both the countries and gave very specific details and names. (Know that even if he had given me the money, this goes against my core values and I would have done the same thing either way.)

At this point, I was preparing strike two:

I was dumb in lending him money, but I least I did it the right way—I wrote a check. I didn't do cash and I wanted proof just in case. It would turn out to be a great idea. On the check, I had written that it was a loan (thank you, Judge Judy, for this tip).

Since he didn't pay me back, I prepared an invoice and sent it to me from his hacked email.

When the time came to do my taxes I filed the loan as an expense using this invoice (I have many freelancers, I slid him as one of them).

And it passed.

Don't ask me how I got his Social Security Number, I can't remember, but I ended up having access to it so I ratted him out to the IRS for hiding income. I found out later on through friends that the IRS started investigating him for unpaid taxed. I heard he had to pay thirty eight percent taxes on that twenty five thousand plus pay a twenty percent fine for not declaring income.

At this point I was satisfied. I figured nine and a half thousand in taxes plus five thousand in fines was half of what he owed me. At least he didn't get away with it all.

But on the check I had written that it was a loan. So it took about two or three years, but I took him to court and won (he didn't even show up). He has to reimburse the full twenty five thousand plus court fees (plus what he owes to the IRS so it's thirty nine and a half thousand that he was to pay for not reimbursing the original twenty five).

To this day I still haven't seen a cent, but the rest of the story makes it worthwhile.

For a long time I thought the financial crime call I made had no effect— now came the cherry on top.

What I didn't know at the time is that the IRS would team up with the

Wire Fraud division and look at *everything* he did.

They were not able to catch him on the wire fraud, but since the house he had did not fit with the money he was declaring they got him on tax evasion and gave him a certain time to pay back taxes (I heard it was only three months, but I don't know if it's accurate).

They got him so good they ended up freezing his accounts, and he *lost his house*. The bank foreclosed it. His debt to the IRS is still open. However we are not in the U.S., so he won't go to jail for this.

My twenty five thousand that he did not want to repay ended up costing him over half a million dollars. Since you cannot go bankrupt for a debt you owe to the government, I'm happy to tell you that at forty he had to move back with his parents and ask for welfare and will probably be paying this for the rest of his life!

I just learned that he now has a job as a concierge in the apartment building of his parents, so I'll be contacting the court to have the money he owes me taken directly from his pay.

The thing is, he has *no* idea I'm the culprit of all his bad fortune and he recently sent me a message telling me he misses me, that I was an angel for him and that he regrets what he did . . .

Well, not me loser, not me!

53

Posted by **Sergnoff**

Greedy aunt served after screwing my family over

I'd like to start with the fact that I live in Russia, and am *not* a good story teller.

This all began about three years ago at my grandma's funeral. She passed away at the age of seventy three, leaving behind three sisters (one of which committed suicide long ago), a plethora of grandkids and quite a lot of real estate.

When the paperwork tsunami regarding the inheritance started, something began to smell fishy.

My aunt was extremely hesitant in giving us the death certificate so we could start filing for inheritance. Things started to get complicated and confusing, so I had to take over all the paperwork and to help my mother out.

Soon I find out that the apartment my grandmother had lived in for some reason no longer belonged to her, and was signed off to the kids of my aunt. Upon further inspection I realized that most of my grandmother's belongings were signed off to my aunt long before my grandmother's death.

First I decided to speak to my mom. She told me that on the date the papers were signed my grandmother was already in pretty bad shape. Dementia and Alzheimer's had already gotten the best of her and she was not legally able to sign them. So I decide to go to my aunt, still not wanting to believe that she screwed us over. I, sincerely believing that it was all an honest deal, ask her how it all happened.

I will never forget her response. I never thought someone could say this to a relative.

She told me that it was none of my business, that she intends to get everything she can and the rest of the real estate that will be shared property she will force us out of.

I was baffled. I couldn't understand how she could do something like this to my mother. I had to do something.

The next day I spoke with my mother. She was shocked and devastated. In tears. She also could not understand how her own sister could do such a thing. Especially after all the things she did for her, like helping her make a career in sports, helping with money during hard times etc. I knew we needed to go to court.

The problem with that was, my mother is a working pensioner and is still raising my thirteen year old brother. I just spent all my savings on renovating her apartment. Money was an issue. Luckily, I made good friends with our company lawyer at work and he offered to help me.

We collected all the necessary paperwork, he told me to document any further encounters with their family and to keep an eye out for anything fishy. After that, we sent a letter to my aunt saying that we will dispute everything in court.

This is where my life became hell.

It all started out with threatening calls from her sons. That's no biggie. I recorded all of the phone conversations. They found out where I work and live and started stalking me. Again, no biggie. A while back my boss made me an offer for a driver to pick me up to and from work because the driver lived near me. About time I hit him up on that offer, so I did.

One morning I wake up and get ready to work. My driver is downstairs waiting for me. I put on a coat and head downstairs. I open the door of my apartment complex and get hit in the face by my oldest cousin. He threatens me again and flees the scene.

The driver runs up, helps me up and tells me that it was all recorded on the car's front cam. He calls my boss and takes me to the hospital. The next day I take the video and all of the phone conversations to the police.

They accept everything.

When the police contacted my aunt, searching for her son that punched me. She was *livid*.

She called me and spat threats in the phone. I reminded her that her son is already in trouble for threatening me. She hangs up.

About a week later I wake up in the middle of the night from loud banging on my door. As I'm walking to the door it gives in and flies open. Two large men walk in, stating this is now their apartment as well.

Handing me the papers they say, "If you want to remain healthy, you should pack your shit and go."

I call the police. They arrive, checks the paperwork and it's totally fine.

Turned out my aunt hired professional . . . erm . . . let's call them "professional inconveniencers"—they make money by forcing people to move out of shared homes.

She gave them a part of her right of ownership and they were legally allowed to move in. Next three months I routinely had to pick my door because they kept changing the lock, had to deal with constant loud music. Dirt and filth in my own house. Barely any sleep.

After three months they gave up and left.

Seeing that this didn't work my cousin's family decided to desperately fuck with me. One night one of them walked in to my apartment complex and started spraying pepper spray at my door to try and lure me out. Unfortunately for him, I was cleaning the house and doing some minor work after the goons they hired. All of my doors were pretty insulated with rags and towels to prevent concrete dust flying everywhere. I barely smelled the pepper spray.

Court was due next day.

I barely convinced my mother to ask for her sister to be eliminated form inhering anything. After I showed the court video and audio of them threatening and assaulting me, it was done. The court ruled in our favor.

Upon returning from court I went to the police to tell them about the pepper spray incident. I was rushed in to a room and questioned.

Turned out my elderly neighbor died from lung complications caused by the pepper spray.

Here I am today, just returned from the notary where my mother signed all the estate to her name. I got a significant amount of money for the assault and threats, and my piece of shit aunt is left with her tiny apartment and a son in prison for assault, threats of violence and homicide. Her second son was fired from the rescue team and is no longer able to work for any government or social structures and he doesn't know how to do anything else.

They're bankrupt, and it serves them right.

54

Posted by **hicctl**

A unique way to share your money among your heirs in a way that is actually fair

This is the story of a good friend of mine's grandfather and how he dealt with his inheritance in a very unique way.

He had two sons, and each of them also had two sons. In the last half year of his life my friend and I visited him every morning and every evening. You see he did not want to go into a retirement home, and apart from getting ready in the morning and in the evening he did not really need help.

Back in the day we still had mandatory service in the army for twelve months, but there was several way around it. I will only explain the most common way, since it is connected to our story. You see instead of going to the army, you could say you refuse to go to the army for ethical reasons (which was really just a formality—you simply wrote a one page essay why you think you being in the army would violate your personal ethics, and they pretty much had to accept it).

But that meant you had to go into civil service.

Civil service could be any kind of job that in a wider sense is a service to society. So these jobs ranged from kindergarten to retirement homes and anything in between like hospitals, homes for the physically or mentally disabled, meals on wheels and pretty much anything you can imagine. You would be paid for that time the same amount of money you would get in the army, and had the right to certain perks like a free room, health insurance, work clothes etc. The same stuff any soldier gets. Plus since soldiers get free food you either got free food or a food allowance.

I did my time in a retirement home, and it was an awesome experience. I think a job like that really widens your horizon as young, arrogant shit and really matures you and shows you what is actually important in life.

I was just done with my time in the retirement home, and for one year simply wanted to job around and make some money. Then one of my best friends comes to me and tells me he needs my help.

His grandpa can no longer do everything by himself, but really only

147

needs help in the morning to get ready and in the evening. Since I have learned how to do this from real professionals, he asks me to show him so his grandpa does not yet have to go into a retirement home. He later admitted grandpa said he would rather kill himself then get into a nursing home, and he seemed really serious about it. He did not tell me at the time since he did not want to pressure me into help like that, which I really appreciated.

He was one of my best friends, and I really liked his grandpa (when I was younger I did not have a grandpa, but we visited him all the time and I became his unofficial fifth grandson) so of course I said yes.

The original plan was to show him for two or three weeks, and then observe him for another two or three weeks and then he would do it on his own. We ended up doing it together for over half a year, then grandpa had a stroke and died within two days in the hospital.

Days later my friend asked me to come with him to the lawyer where the last will would be read. His grandfather had specifically asked that his will should be read the day before he gets buried, which is quite unusual, but not illegal as such. I asked why he wanted me there, and my friend told me the lawyer had officially invited me since grandpa had left me something as a thank you for my service.

I was a bit embarrassed, but also happy that grandpa had thought so highly of my service he even put me in his last will.

Now my friend's dad is an entitled asshole and the same goes for his uncle. We arrived there and went into the room, and his father turned to me. "Why the hell are you here? I know that dad called you in jest his fifth grandkid, but this is for real family."

"I bet the little gold digger hoped he would get some money in the will," the uncle muttered.

I took a breath. "I was asked to be here by the lawyer. Take it up with him, I have no idea why I am here."

"If you pulled something to get to his money I will sue you so hard even your kids will still need lawyers!" the father shouted threateningly.

"Show some respect and stop shouting," my friend said, jumping in. "I know you two did not really give a shit about your dad, but show at least a minimum of respect."

The uncle scoffed. "How dare you talk like that to your elders you little shit?"

"You two get exactly as much respect from me as you showed your own father *none*." My friend really shouted the last word, and it finally shut the two up.

We sat down and still had to wait for the other grand kids to arrive. They sat right behind us, and what they talked about really made my blood boil.

Apparently they had both gotten new cars, new jewelry for their wives and had planned a huge holiday. All that was paid for by credit and they had planned to pay for it with the inheritance. None of them said even a word about missing him, being sad that he died. *Nothing.*

Only me, me, me, me and money, money, money.

They seemed to be in competition—who could spend the inheritance faster the way they planned away the money.

Then finally we were all there and the lawyer read out a short letter. What I tell you here is a much shortened version, but the real thing was several pages. But it boils down to this:

In recent years I realized more and more that some people in my family cared a lot more about me than others. I am especially disappointed in my two sons, but I wanted to be really fair and not biased, so I came up with a point system.

Letter or phone call: 1 point + 1 extra if it is very long
Visit: 2 points per hour plus 1 point per hour of travel to me and back
Helping me out with something: 3 points per hour

This is the final result over the last three years of my life:

The Entitled Dad: 8 points
The Entitled Uncle: 10 points
Entitled Kid 1: 150 points
Entitled Kid 2: 133 points
My Friend's brother: 288 points
My friend: 7341
And, me (the author): 5883

My lawyer has already liquidated most of my assets except the house. Once it is sold, the money will be divided by the points so we know what each point is worth, and then every person gets a share of the money according to his points.

For about a minute you could hear a pin drop, then both the dad and uncle started shouting at the same time that they knew we would have pulled something and this will would never stand.

Of course they tried to sue (all of them on one side), but they lost and there was a secret clause (not really secret, it was simply not read to us that day, so nobody realized it was in there since we all assumed everything was read to us on that day by the lawyer) in the will that if someone sues against the will he loses his share of the inheritance.

It took nearly three years until all the lawsuits where over.

I was blown away when we finally got the money. I am not naming a sum, but it was way more then I felt comfortable accepting so I wanted to give at least some of it to the other three grandkids. My friend finally convinced me to accept. "You cared for him when he needed you, without expecting anything for it which makes you ten times more his family than any of those fuckers. They got what they deserved."

55

Posted by **TanyaSapien**

The neighborhood remembers. The neighborhood punishes.

To set the stage, I used to live in a big but not huge city. Let's call it Palmville. I lived near the corner of a dense suburb nestled between overstuffed apartment buildings, a river that smelled like diesel when at low tide and two busy highways.

I was a minority in this neighborhood and I caught a lot of heat for it. People didn't really like white people there, but enough of our neighbors were accepting of us that aside from a few disagreements between families and the beatings that came with them I didn't feel like I was in danger when leaving my home. It was a rough neighborhood, but it was my home and it protected its own.

The Community Center was like a temple, and Amy was the priestess. In our neighborhood she was respected like a living deity, and her calm and understanding reflected her status. I never once saw her behave without a strong moral code.

And the final piece to set this stage, our former landlord. A short Asian lady in all the stereotypical ways—kind and sweet. Our house was above my parent's pay grade and she knew it. She went out of her way to find house repair and maintenance jobs for tenants that were having money problems. She'd pay them by taking chunks out of their rent, often times a bit larger than how much the work they did was worth.

Looking back, that was probably illegal but that's irrelevant because she died. The circumstances surrounding her death were suspect, but none of the suspects play a part in this story so there's no need to go into detail on it.

Her sons, who wanted nothing to do with real-estate, took over the business. They couldn't make heads or tails of how she managed to float books with so much red in them and began dumping properties. Ours was on that list. I harbor no ill-will towards them, and still wish them the best but the guy who bought the house . . . enter the sociopath and today's victim.

This guy wasted no time in making our lives hell.

His first action was to raise the rent. Apparently when the account changed hands, he was allowed to update the rent to modern pricing. We'd been there for several years and were paying below market even from the onset, so this was a huge blow by itself.

The second blow came when he said that the rent had to be ready, in full, on the first of every month—no partial payments, no work to reduce it, no extensions. Full rent on the first of the month or an eviction notice on the second. This was hemorrhaging our savings, but we were surviving for the moment.

Meanwhile, Amy had lobbied hard for the city to co-fund a revival project to renovate the entire aging suburb and she succeeded. One street at a time had conga lines of work trucks almost every day and people were getting old leaky pipes replaced, sinkholes in yards patched, fences repaired, paint renewed. It was an amazing thing, and an enticing thing for the sociopath.

Being on the corner of the neighborhood our house was on the last street on the list, and the sociopath wanted us out so he could relist the house after renovation. He never said this directly, but multiple conversations made his intent clear even for ten year old me.

Random inspections, overhyping of minor problems with the house— even so far as trying to bring us up on completely false animal abuse charges because our cat was attacked by what we believe was a raccoon and he tried to claim we did it.

Yeah, because a vet can't figure out the difference between knife wounds and a mauling.

We read the writing on the wall and began preparations to move. We decided to move in with my oldest brother in a place I'll call Banjoland. Most of us had moved except my other brother, who stayed behind because he still had a lot of social ties in Palmville and his new job meant if he cut corners, he could keep paying sociopath's inflated bills.

Well, despite his best efforts my brother came up twenty dollars short one month and the sociopath jumped on it. He had thirty days to vacate.

We made the four hundred mile trip from Banjoland to Palmville to get the rest of our stuff and I can't say as I approved of my brother's living conditions, but I guess that's beside the point. The month passed rather uneventfully—I guess the sociopath figured he'd won so there was no need to burn the gas to drive out and gloat.

During this turmoil the neighborhood had learned what was going on and that was the first time I'd ever been back in that neighborhood where I didn't get a single callout, a single glare or a single racist remark. Everybody behaved reverently. It was kind of disturbing in all honesty. I guess people in lower income areas all know what eviction means and felt like I was having a bad enough time already.

Well, twenty days later the sociopath says it's time to leave. We still had a week left, but it didn't matter—we didn't have the money to try fighting it with a lawyer.

Then Amy descended from the heavens and bought us a couple extra days, but it was evident he really, really wanted us out—possibly because the work trucks were now one street away.

The last time I ever saw the house I grew up in, workmen were throwing my childhood possessions into a large bin when we supposedly still had three days left to leave.

Everything that follows is a collection of information I got through the grapevine and phone calls with people present at the events.

Immediately, the sociopath moved into the house himself. Why you may ask? People who owned the homes they were living in were getting the full cost of renovations comped by the city. He figured that by moving in himself, he'd be able to get this house he bought at liquidation price renovated for free and flip it.

Amy was having none of it.

She explained to him that at the time the revival project was approved, that house was a rental lot and they can't change the budget now. She then explained to him that the partial cost coverage that had been approved for the lot was in our name, not his, and he wasn't eligible for partial cost comping either.

He'd have to pay every penny himself, and since the entire neighborhood was getting a facelift he was required to at least renovate the exterior, otherwise she'd see the house condemned as an eyesore or dilapidated or whatever the legal term is.

He went really cheap on the renovations, basically put in new carpets and a coat of paint.

This would later come to bite him in the ass.

He then began trying to sell the house in earnest. The neighborhood remembered what he'd done. There were vandalisms when nobody was there, and loud noises from the neighbors when people were there to look the house over. Anytime a prospective buyer asked around, they got the full stink eye from anybody they talked to. They made sure he simply couldn't get that house sold at market value.

After three months of this he lowered the listing price. Then a month later he lowered it again and finally got a bite.

Amy personally made sure he had to file *every single piece* of paperwork before it changed hands. Every single part of the house had to be inspected thoroughly.

And that's when Karma herself caught up with him. In his hasty and cheap renovations, he'd somehow damaged the pipes.

Black Mold.

Amy remembered how he'd treated us and she decided to pay him back in kind.

I never heard how exactly she pulled it off, but she managed to delay him getting the news about the black mold being discovered for several days, long enough that by time he did get the news he didn't have enough time left to try getting it cleaned or make a last ditch effort to save the house.

The house was condemned days later.

In their final act, Amy and members of the neighborhood filed every single complaint and injunction they could and arranged for him to be compelled by the city to demolish the house immediately. A cost he had to pay out of his own pocket.

He tried to destroy a family and broke laws just to make some quick cash, and instead was left fighting a year long legal battle and ended up losing thousands.

The neighborhood remembers. The neighborhood punishes.

56

"In my 35 years of being in sales and sales management that was by far the most interesting performance review I have ever witnessed"

I was working with a business to business sales company (we sold services to companies basically), and this company had managed to hire the most incompetent, lazy and jealous sales manager I have ever come across.

We were a team of five sales people and a sales manager—all five of us sales people hated our sales manager for various reasons, but we liked her personally.

I was the top sales person on the team, sitting at one hundred and seventy percent of my yearly objective and was well on my way to the presidents club. This is largely because I was the only sales person on the team with real sales experience and the sales manager was too incompetent to train a team.

My VP came down for our yearly performance reviews and I was called in first. It was my VP and the sales manager Mrs. B (short for Bitch). I was expecting a positive performance review.

Right off the bat Mrs. B hits me with, "Sting, you know our location hasn't been performing at objective for a number of years and we suspect this is because sales people are misrepresenting their daily work."

I'm taken aback.

"Sting I don't think you are actually doing what you say you are doing in your CRM. This is something that could get you fired."

I later found out Mrs. B was on a six month plan—she either got the location numbers up or was going be fired. I guess she wanted to play hardball. The thing is, she played hardball with the wrong person.

I looked at Mrs. B and I said "Really?"

She replied with "Yea."

"I'm shocked you decided to go this route," I replied.

Mrs. B put on a confident smile. "We gotta do what it takes to get this location on objective."

"Alright, I said, "Let's play a game. Mrs. B, pick a day. Any day in the CRM and let me prove to you that I went to all my appointments and did all my stops as recorded."

"Well Sting, I'm not saying you never go in the field. I just think some days you stay at home and put in BS notes in the CRM."

"Mrs. B, pick a day—any day. Pick a day you think I lied about my sales activities."

So Mrs. B picks a day, and I'm smiling ear to ear. I notice the VP is smiling at me and his head is slanted to one side.

I suspected he knew Mrs. B was about to get absolutely fucking owned . . . and he was right.

I turn to the VP. "Are you aware of how Android phones work?"

"Enlighten me."

"By default Android has location services turned on, and in fact Google will track where you went and when. Naturally I carry my phone everywhere, so let's compare what Google says I did that day to what my CRM says." I pull up my google location services for that day, and surprise, surprise, it's a match.

Mrs. B is obviously very concerned at this point.

"I'm actually quite enjoying this performance review, I said casually, "let's pick another day Mrs. B."

"We don't need to do that," she fires back.

I turn to the VP again. "Would you mind picking a day?"

"Sure, what about XYZ?" she says, pulling up my CRM and I pull the location services for that day.

Guess what? It's a match.

I then get ready to pull out the big guns. "Mr. VP, do you remember company XYZ with a contract value in excess of one million dollars that we lost recently?"

"Yes Sting, I remember. Apparently our competitor won them over on price. We can't win them all."

I nodded. "Here is an email from *their* VP basically stating that they've decided not to go with us for our failure to provide three samples for them to decide on which product worked best for them."

"Sting can you forward that to me?" he asks.

"Sure, not a problem," I reply and do just that. "While I'm at this, let me forward you over several email chains before this where I clearly asked Mrs. B to order those samples. In fact in those very same email chains she confirmed that had in fact ordered the samples." He asked me to forward those emails to him so I did.

"Now Mr. VP I had our service department look to see if any orders had been placed for those samples," I continued. "No orders were actually placed."

"I'm going look into this," he said after receiving it all.

Mrs. B is sweating bullets at this point. My performance review has just turned into her performance review and shit's not going right.

"I have one more thing I'd like to bring to your attention," I said. "Do you mind if I step outside for a minute so I can show you?"

"Sure," he replied. "I need to have a talk with Mrs. B anyway."

Several years prior to this a general manager at another location raped a woman. The company was sued and lost a lot of money because of this. Since this incident the company put in a very clear cut policy of "no sexual relations between management and people who work for them". It's immediate termination for the manager.

Another sales consultant in the office, Joe, was a married man with two beautiful kids and Mrs. B had the hots for him. She tried to have sex with him multiple times, twice over text. Joe and I had talked about if he should report this transgression.

I walked into the sales office and said, "Joe, I think it's time we get a new sales manager. You still got those texts?"

He looks at me. "Is today going be the day?"

"Today is going be the day," I replied.

All the sales staff knew what was going on—the mood in the office was lifted. Joe and I begin walking back to the conference room when the location manager who was not a part of the performance review saw Joe and me.

"What's going on?" he asked.

"You're going need to hire a new sales manager soon" Joe replied.

The location manager was confused and said he's coming in to the meeting to which we said fine. I knocked on the door and we were told to come in.

There we stood, Joe, the location manager and myself. Mrs. B knew exactly what was about to happen. We all took our seats, and I turned to the VP. "I just want to clarify a company policy."

"Sure."

"Is it true that if a manager tried to engage in a sexual relationship with someone under them that it's immediate termination for that manager?"

Mr. VP sits up straight, takes a moment and replies, "Yes, if something like that came to my attention my hands would be tied. I'd have to fire the manager."

"Well Joe has something he wants to show you."

Mrs. B got up and walked out of the conference room. You could tell she was about to cry. Her world, her career, had just completely wrecked and I don't think she wanted to be around for the end.

Joe went on to tell the VP how he's a happily married man with two beautiful kids and Mrs. B kept hitting on him. In fact she had sent him numerous sexual texts, and on two occasions openly invited him to come have sex with her—once in the office and once at his home even after he had made it clear he wasn't going have sex with her.

Mr. VP asked to see the texts and Joe provided them.

The VP asked him to screen shot those and email them over, then the VP said, "I'm going need both of you to go back to the sales office. The location manager and I have some talking to do"

We walk back into the sales office and I notice the sales manager office looked cleaned out. Apparently Mrs. B was a wreck and crying before saying she was going home.

Joe laughed. "Yea, she won't be coming back."

It was about twenty five minutes later when the VP came into the sales office and asked me to come to the conference room again. I sat down and the VP cleared his throat. "Well, I would like to inform you that Mrs. B has been terminated effectively immediately. With that being said, after your performance review and looking over your numbers you are our top sales rep in this location. You deserve nothing short of stellar remarks on your review and you'll be getting that."

"Thank you. I do have one question though?"

"Sure, anything."

"How do I apply for new sales manager job that just opened up?"

Mr. VP chuckled. "You sure do you like to strike while the iron is hot don't you?"

I said I do, and he assured me he would let the location manager know and I'd be able to put in my application. I thanked him and he shook his head. "No, thank you. In my thirty five years of being in sales and sales management that was by far the most interesting performance review I have ever witnessed."

I did not end up getting promoted and quit shortly after this because they decided to not promote me and instead hired a guy with no sales experience to be our sales manager. This rubbed me the wrong way.

Also, our service department sucked and couldn't deliver on what I was selling. Another company offered me more money.

57

Posted by **personaldistance**

Call me a terrorist and threaten my pay? Enjoy your nuked careers, yuh heathens.

I used to work in hospitality in a metro known for its obscenely huge tourist population, you know, the city built around the Mouse.

I was a manager for the recreational division of the hotel. So one day, my boss (who we'll call Mary for the purpose of the story), comes into the shared manager's office and while rummaging around for something strikes up a small conversation about work related minutiae with me. It's important to note she is actually two tiers above me, but was acting as head of the department while searching to replace my previous boss who recently quit (great guy by the way, huge loss to the company).

As we're talking, she abruptly stops and says, "By the way, you need to shave your beard. You look like a terrorist and I don't employ terrorists."

Haha. Funny joke between colleagues, right? Nope.

I am half Indian and I do look middle-eastern, and I have been taking this kind of shit since middle school. Plus, we're not close, at all.

So I reply as calmly as I can muster, "Hey, I get you're trying to be funny, but on my end it comes off as pretty ignorant so I'd appreciate it if you chilled out with the terrorist stuff."

"Oh, I'm ignorant?" Mary Retorts. "We'll see how ignorant I am during your annual review," and proceeds to walk out of the room in a huff.

My jaw dropped so low I could taste the floor.

You would think it was an easy fix, right? Go to HR and all. She's made rude comments like this before. I've refrained from contacting HR because I didn't want to be petty, but now she threatened my pay and that's *no bueno*.

So I go to HR like a good boy and tell the HR director, who we'll call Boyd. I explicitly ask him not to mention it to anyone—just to log it away in case someone else reports something similar and he can establish a pattern of behavior. Well, Boyd decided that he simply must talk to Mary about it.

I stress again that I am not comfortable with it, since she strikes me as the vindictive type. No good. He promises there will be no retaliation and tells me he'll contact me later for a statement (which I thought was weird, why not make a statement now?) and that was that.

About a week goes by and I follow up with Boyd because I've been getting some less-than-pleasant vibes from Mary. Nothing substantial, but odd.

"Well it appears that Mary was just joking," he said, "but she has agreed to never say anything like that again. Your annual review is not in jeopardy."

. . . Oooooooook.

At that point, I decide to just let it go. Fast forward a month, a new director for our department is hired and surprise, surprise—it's her roommate and former front desk supervisor, "Joe".

Ok, cool. I'm used to the nepotism because the entire hotel basically operates that way. Whatever. Never had an issue with him, didn't know him too well but I'm happy our little hive has a leader again.

Man, how fucking naive I was.

From the get go he is unpleasant. Snide comments left and right, changing my schedule at the last minute every week or scheduling me on my established days off. Giving away opportunities to my peers that I'm never considered for. Making me take "improvement classes" none of my peers have to take. All strange but up to that point nothing "earth-shattering".

Until one day I get written up out of the blue (first ever write up by the way) for "refusing to inform a superior of leaving the premises", referring to me leaving the day prior without literally saying the words "Hey Joe, I'm leaving for the day".

First off, this is not an established policy written or otherwise. When I say I'm leaving, it's a courtesy.

Secondly I know for a *fact* my peers don't always say when they leave (personal observation), and this was corroborated by them after asking around.

Thirdly, knowing that my peers aren't held to the same bogus standard, *and* having never been written up for it, I know this is a direct shot at me. My review is fucked. Best part—Joe let it slip that *Mary* asked for me after I left and when it was found that I was indeed gone, she *requested* the write-up. That was fuck up number two, lady.

My third came when Boyd decided to cover his own ass when I approached him with all the evidence pointing to retaliation and discrimination in the workplace. I learned he never properly documented his discussion with me or Mary, and that he's been basically playing the whole fucking thing by ear.

I decided to write my long past due statement then and there, turn it in and e-mail a picture copy to the corporate office. I tell Boyd that I am sorely disappointed about how he handled the issue and he responds by accusing me of "dramatizing" the whole ordeal. He was very flippant about the whole thing, rolling his eyes and everything.

Okay, buddy. I see you now.

After some time, I scrounge up all the evidence I can. My write-up, my co-workers write-up records (with their permission), company policy manuals, my schedules for the past month (including the bogus classes only I was made to attend), my co-workers schedules, witness statements (from peers when Mary has said other demeaning things) and a few others items.

Next step, I tell off Joe—because fuck him. I make sure he is *very* angry when I leave. You'll see why later.

After crossing my T's and dotting my I's, I resigned with a two week notice.

That night, I type up a letter to the EEOC and attach all my evidence. I mention Mary, Boyd and Joe by first and last name. I hint that I am pondering a lawsuit. A few weeks later, I have my girlfriend call my old job pretending to be a potential employer asking for a reference. I give her the extension to Joe's desk.

As I predicted, he slanders the ever-loving shit out of me (straight up lies, even got my resignation date wrong along with my attendance record—all verifiable, helping my case). I tried the same trick with Boyd, but he was smart enough to point my girlfriend in the direction of a third party reference dialer the company is supposed to use for these kinds of calls. I proceed to send my old employer (corporate included) a Cease and Desist letter with a transcript of the call, hinting I may sue for slander.

More time passes, and the other day I'm at the bank with my girlfriend when I get a call from an old co-worker. I miss the call, but I resign to call him back later.

Less than an hour later I get five or six calls and texts informing me that Mary, Joe, and Boyd were all fired the same day and were walked out of the building.

Mary cried.

Apparently, the corporate office was contacted by the EEOC and launched their own internal investigation, matching their records with my evidence. The EEOC sent me a return letter with the companies statement, which was fallacious as fuck (due to their interviews with the three stooges), but nonetheless I suppose they decided it was easier to nip it in the bud and sack their asses to be safe.

Karma may be a bitch, but in this case, she had nothing to fuckin' do with it.

IF YOU ENJOYED THESE STORIES THEN DON'T FORGET TO
CHECK OUT REDDIT.COM AND LOOK FOR THE
R/ENTITLEDPARENTS
R/CHOOSINGBEGGARS AND
R/PROREVENGE
SUBREDDITS FOR MANY, MANY MORE

www.ingramcontent.com/pod-product-compliance
Lightning Source LLC
Chambersburg PA
CBHW021125020426
42331CB00005B/638